Echo Fall! Report while
painting the forrest floor!
Autumnal vignettes—rust, orange and gold
Your homelands' story lay chronicled.

So too do tears leave,
Newton's code ever boundless,
From twig to ground
same thought to cheek.

Each tiny portal,
its lineage clear—
Set the stage
for Sorrows pulpit!

B.P. BRAWDY

SOMETHING TO
Believe IN

B.P. Brawdy
Creator of Mind-Ups[SM]

MIND
WISE LTD

CHICAGO • ILLINOIS

Grateful acknowledgement is made to the following for permission to reprint previously published material:

W.W. Norton & Company, Inc.: Excerpts from *Man's Search For Himself*, copyright 1953 by Rollo May. Reprinted by permission.

Published by MindWise Ltd.
401 West Ontario • Suite 220 • Chicago, Illinois 60610
mindwise1@aol.com

Library of Congress Catalog Card Number: 97-93991
ISBN 0-9658937-4-X
First Edition by Author
Printed in the United States of America
Cover design by Lisa Eckert

The publisher has made every attempt to obtain the proper permissions for the reprinting of copyrighted material. We will graciously add to our list of permissions in future additions.
10 9 8 7 6 5 4 3 2 1

Dedicated to
Alex and Sean Griffin.
For reasons you will grow to understand.

In memory of John B. Blydenburgh

困

ACKNOWLEDGMENTS

First and foremost, I thank Terri Griffin, without whose continual support and encouragement this project would not have been possible; Thanks Bud!

A special thank you to my wife Liz for her understanding and patience. Thanks to Robert and Mary Varese. Thanks to Carl and Corine Sandstrom. A heart felt thank you to Marcy L. Rice for being there when I needed you. Thanks to Joseph Zednick for the call to "take this show on the road" and to Martin Israel and family at Meyersons for never doubting the successful completion of STBI. Thanks to Josh Mintz and family for always believing. Special thanks also to Janice Czechowicz and John Brawdy, from the very beginning.

Thanks to Dr. Patricia Katherine Novick for her thoughts and for the forward of this book, Dr. Dharma Singh Khalsa for his guidance and to Marilynn Preston for her years of guidance and challenging words. Hey, Lisa Eckert, thanks so much for your creative touch and inspiration, to Tom Cronin for the extra push and to Leticia Herrera for your thoughts. Thanks also to Reggie Tillery, Larry Fleming, Elaine and Molly Pontello. Also, thanks to Dennis Walto, Noel Boxer, Bob Kelty, and Craig Kulaszewski.

Thanks to Bart and Sue Brawdy and Brett and Terri Brawdy. Thanks to Dr. Mitchel and Sharon Sheinkop for bringing me to Chicago in the first place. Thanks to Rob and Erica Drager and Patty Higgins. To Llyod P., Rick E., Claire S., and Janice B.. You know why.

A sincere thank you to Howard and Gayle at Transitions Bookplace in Chicago.

Thanks to Paul Alfred Brawdy for the lesson.

It would not be fair to exclude the following authors, for although we have never met, I am in great debt to them for their help. Joseph Campbell, Carl Jung, Lao-tzu, Socrates, Plato, Shakespeare, Jesus, Buddha, Thoreau, Emerson, Goethe, Kafka, Nietzsche, Gandhi, Helen Keller, Abhram Maslow, W. Sommerset Maugham, John Bartlett, Wayne Dwyer, Depak Chopra, W.B. Yeats, William Wordsworth, William James, Albert Camus, Isaac Asimov, Cervantes, Maya Angelou, Fritjof Capra, Howard Gardner, Charles Darwin, T.S. Eliot, Albert Einstein, Mircea Eliade, Will and Ariel Durant, Frederick Copleston, Houston Smith, Emile Durkheim, P.D. Mehta, Buckminster Fuller, Robert Frost, Thomas Mann, Arthur Schopenhauer, Ortega y Gasset, Frederick Douglas, Paul Brunton, Kahlil Gibran, Kabir, Rumi, Ram Das, Thich Nhat Hanh, Krishnamurti, Aldous Huxley, Michelangelo, Picasso, Ludwig van Beethoven, Alighieri Dante, Emily Dickinson, John Donne and James Joyce for self-publishing Ulysses.

To the learner in You and to the One.

FORWARD

This book is about learning: learning about oneself, learning how best to be an authentic person in a world that throws up obstacle after obstacle to our being so, and learning how to learn.

I had known Brian for just a relatively short time when I invited him to my wedding celebration, which was attended principally by friends I had known for many years. The celebration was informal; there was no best man, hence no one designated to offer the wedding toast. When the time came for that toast, everyone hesitated self-consciously to step forward and offer it.

Everyone, that is, except Brian, who put his arms around my husband and me and delivered an oration that had the attendees in tears, so beautiful was its evocation of the glory of life and the power of love.

That's Brian, who has learned about what matters and who, as you will see, knows how to communicate it.

The best definition of learning that I've seen appears in a delightful article by David Boulton in *The Music Trades* magazine. Boulton writes, "Whether for knowing, doing, or being, learning is a process of extending the capability to be relevantly present to what is being experienced." You'll find in this book much that will help you accomplish that kind of leaning, but I think Brian's message also goes farther, because it teaches us how to use learning to change the ways in which we see things and approach the world. To go from the bundle of apprehension and guilt that he once was to the sunburst of joy that he is now is no small step, not just a change but a wholesale transformation.

So, the gift that Brian gives us here is a compelling story of the ways in which we integrate learning into our approach to the world—how we construct and reconstruct our reality. Columbia's Jack Mezirow writes of individuals' *meaning perspectives*—their "sets of habits of expectation...which serve as selective codes governing perception and comprehension." Meaning perspectives provide the framework within which individuals interpret experience, solve problems, acquire information, and remember. They are usually tacit, rather that explicit. Part of Brian's genius is to make explicit, for all of us, perceptions that often remain tacit, influencing our behavior outside of our conscious awareness.

Transformative learning of the sort Brian describes here—learning which make new meaning—occurs when meaning perspectives are changed. The primary function of meaning perspectives is to organize the barrage of information which we receive every day into patterns by which that information is assimilated and understood. There is a relationship between the information and the meaning perspective. Sometimes the information fits neatly into an existing framework; sometimes it is adapted or modified (consciously or unconsciously) to fit a preexisting framework; and sometimes the framework is adapted or modified to accommodate the new information. Most of the time, the basic meaning perspective remains intact—people continue to understand the world much as they did before. At other times, it may be necessary to adopt a new, different perspective.

Along with Gregory Bateson, Erving Goffman, and others, Mezirow has speculated on the ways in which learning may become transformative. He says that reflection, the act of becoming aware of *"why* we attach the meanings we do to reality, especially to our roles and relationships…may be the most significant distinguishing characteristic of adult learning."

Reflection sounds relaxed and easy, like something you might do with a fishing pole in hand on a lazy summer afternoon. Brian show how tough it can be, examining things one might rather set aside, looking into the sun for the penumbral shapes that provide it with definition.

That he forced himself, in order to survive as a vibrant and alive person, to learn skills of seeing is evident from these pages. That his vision for things large and small, light and dark, remains intensely acute today is also obvious, not only from his lucid writing but from the way he handles his day-to-day interactions. The effort to see truly, that is, has a long-term payoff even greater than its short-run benefits.

As we all learn more about learning, as our confidence grows that we have the capacity to find solid solutions to our most wrenching challenges, perhaps we will concurrently achieve better ways to achieve the kind of transcendent holism Brian adumbrates here: a deep knowledge of one's connection with all other elements. Such perspectives can be traced back at least as far as the

Upanishad, twenty-five centuries ago. In that view, "self" is "the anonymous center, the realest of realities". The following words express transcendent holism:

Self is everywhere, shining forth from all beings,
vaster than the vast, subtler that the most subtle,
unreachable, yet nearer than breath, than heartbeat.
Eye cannot see it, ear cannot hear it nor tongue
utter it: only in deep absorption can the mind,
grown pure and silent, merge with the formless truth.

As soon as you have found it,
you are free you have found yourself,
you have solved the great riddle,
your heart forever at peace.
Whole, you enter the whole, Your personal self
returns to its radiant, intimate, deathless source.

In this moving book, we all learn a lot about the finding of that radiant self.

Patricia Katherine Novick, Ph.D.

AUTHOR'S NOTE

As a first time author, I initially made a mistake that would only become apparent to me at the completion of the final edit of Something To Believe In.

My error was one based on inexperience and naiveté. While sitting at my first attempt of this book, I decided to write the "Forward" prior to the contents of the book itself.

In that first section, I set out to apologize to the would-be reader for my "Cop/Detective like mentality" and for the "Investigative tone" of which I had adopted.

I rambled on about my "only education being that which I had received from the Police Academy in New York" and lamented my "lack of any institutionalized learning."

Upon completion of Something To Believe In, the sorrowful feeling was gone. At books end, it was glaringly apparent that for anyone bent on discovering the true meaning of their life, all they had to rely upon thankfully, not apologetically was that which had been the focus of their life heretofore.

How does the old saying go? "You gotta dance with the one you came with." The moment one sets out to discover their Something To Believe In, all that has come before is all that you can count on. All past experience, knowledge and circumstance becomes the fuel for your personal truth quest. The past holds no shame, only fuel to the future.

What is "truth" and how does one find it? The major focus of this book sets out to answer the above question. For now, there is a one word answer that I believe will suffice.

The Ancient Greek word for "truth" is *aletheia* which literally translates as "the unmasked" or the "unhidden." Suppose for a second, that truth lies within you and that it need only be uncovered in order to be realized? Imagine just for a moment-that your *Something To Believe In* is concealed or hidden in the opaqueness of your daily struggle for survival. How then would you act?

Throughout the remaining pages of this book, you will be called upon to investigate your own beliefs, to interrogate your long held thoughts and many of the "mental fancies" that you currently possess. In the end you will be called upon to make an "arrest."

My search led me through the fields of Philosophy, Psychology, the Sciences, Comparative Religion and Mythology. I reviewed the written testimonies of Plato, Jung, Einstein, Houston Smith, Joseph Campbell and many more. Your investigation may-or may not depending upon your preference-lead you in a similar direction. Only your time will tell.

For sure, you will certainly find that the techniques that I employed as a criminal investigator in a New York police agency will be equally as powerful a tool for you during your own personal search.

As a cop, my search for evidence and clues led to a conviction in court. Your search will lead to a "conviction of the heart." Your journey will lead to the "arrest" of your own *Something To Believe In.*

CHAPTER I

The Fall

•

*Life means to have something to do a mission
to fulfill-and in the measure in which we avoid setting
our life to something, we make it empty. Human life, by
its very nature has to be dedicated to something, an
enterprise glorious or humble, a destiny
illustrious or trivial.*

—JOSE ORTEGA Y GASSET

困

Just about a decade ago now, I began my personal
search for *Something to Believe In*. The year was 1987
and President Reagan and Mikhail Gorbechav signed a
treaty to eliminate their countries' medium range nuclear
missiles.

A young superstar named Michael Jordan would
become only the second player in the history of the
National Basketball Association-Wilt Chamberlain
being the first-to score 3000 points in a single season.

Black Monday rumbled nation wide, when the Dow
Jones lost almost 1/4 of its value and fell more than 500
points in a single day.

This particular year found me as a police officer. I had been recently promoted to the position of Criminal Detective and assigned to a Federal Drug Enforcement Task Force in New York.

Life seemed to be progressing nicely. I had graduated at the top of my Police Academy class, received numerous letters of commendation and was the youngest patrolman to be promoted to detective in the history of my department.

For the first time in my life I was in charge, and it went straight to my head. No one could tell me anything, I knew it all. That was until the intercom announced, "Detective Brawdy, you have an incoming phone call on line three."

Tapping the flashing light third from the left I answered, "Detective Brawdy."

"Brian?" The voice questioned.

"This is Detective Brawdy. Who's speaking?"

When the answer came my gun and badge did little to protect me.

"Brian, it's me, Paul."

"Paul who?"

It had been a long time since I had last heard the voice of my father.

"It's me, your dad."

The penetrating rush of emotion was so great, that movement-let alone speech-was all but impossible. It had been fifteen years since my father had left us and I had forgotten the sound of his voice. I sat frozen in my chair.

"Brian, I know its been a quite awhile but I still think

of you and your mom a lot. I was in hopes of maybe getting together if you'd like."

I sat without replying, too stunned to speak.

"Are you still there?"

"Yea" was all I could muster.

"Well, what do ya' think? I'd really like to see you."

I was stupefied-all the memories of pain and the feelings of paternal abandonment played front and center in my mind. There had been birthday parties, elementary school spelling bees, little league soccer debuts and even a trip to the emergency room. Nothing I could do would bring him home. Each day I thought, "Today is the day that my dad will come home." Rejection always seems worst when your alone late at night. As a young boy, I spent many lonely evenings crying myself to sleep, always wondering if I had done something to drive him away. Had I "been a bad boy?"

My father, a seasoned alcoholic-and no doubt the reason I grew up needing the implied authority of a badge and a gun in order to feel in control of my life-left home when I was very young. He took the family car, the minimal savings account and left my Mom with five little kids and no food in the fridge; she worked three jobs just so we could survive.

Finally, after all those years there was definitely a valid target for what seemed to be limitless amounts of my frustration and anger. Almost as if by evil possession, the torture of my early years was overtaken by the desire for revenge.

My inability to speak was replaced with alternating

waves of fury and rage. Like a forest fire out of control, my anger would not be contained. After all this time my penalty could be exacted on the one who truly deserved to be punished.

Lashing out over the phone, I demanded, "Where the hell have you been all along?"

With a voice more reflective of a growl I continued, "Are you nuts? Do you really think that after all this time you can just decide to be a dad and that squares us? You can just pick up the damn phone after all these years, like we've never missed a beat? What's with you anywise?"

There was silence on the line.

"Let me see if I've got this straight. I...I wan'ta make sure that I'm hearing you correctly. Are you telling me that after fifteen Christmas's you've finally decided to spend this year's holiday with your oldest son? Is that what your telling me?"

"Brian, I know it's been..."

Before he could finish I barked, "Look, you don't know a damn thing about me or how I feel. For all I care you can just drop dead."

"Brian..."

I slammed the phone down on the receiver. I didn't want to hear anything he had to say. His explanation would cure nothing. His reasons could do little to quell the inferno.

The rest of the day was spent inflating my chest and bragging-to anyone who would listen-about how I had finally evened the score. It was the perfect Christmas present to myself. Revenge did indeed fill my mouth with a sweet taste. Finally, he had been taught what it felt like to be abandoned during the holidays. Tough luck, huh?

I still had the power, I was still in control-at least so I thought. The events of the following week would prove to me just how wrong I truly was.

It was late in the evening and my pager went off. My girlfriend and I were just leaving her office Christmas party. The last thing I wanted to do was to go to the office. The message was marked "Urgent, 10-43; return to station." Be grudgingly, I dropped Elise off and headed for the P.D..

A Sergeant was waiting in the door way when I arrived . He did not seem pleased as he paced back and forth. My mind began to race. Sergeants only call you in when you've screwed up. What could it be? Had I done something wrong, was there a civilian complaint, had I screwed up a case?

"Brian I have some terrible news for you." His expression and tone made it clear that he would rather be somewhere else.

"What's up Sarge?" I asked with a nervous twinge in my stomach.

His reply was quick and curt.

"I just received a phone call from 12th Precinct Homicide and they need to speak with you A.S.A.P."

He handed me a piece of paper with a detective's name and number written in black ink.

Looking up from the note I shrugged my shoulders and asked, "What the hell do they want this late at night?"

"Brian...it's your father, he's dead. I'm really sorry. If there is anything I can do, please let me know?"

"He's dead? How did it happen?" My racing mind saturated with possible scenarios. The Sergeant looked down.

"He committed suicide, Brian." There was a long pause.

"The detectives say he jumped from the roof of his apartment building. They need you to go downtown to identify his body. I really am sorry Brian. Are you OK to drive? I'll have a patrolman take you back home if you'd like."

"No thanks. I'll be all right" I replied, cupping my forehead in the palm of my right hand. My thoughts were of our last conversation.

The drive home was the longest two miles of my life. With the exception of a burning gut, total numbness set in. Had the long remembered hurt and pain justified my actions on the phone? Had he taken me seriously when I told him to "drop dead?" As a youngster, he had always ignored me whenever I would ask him not to leave. Why had he chosen to listen to me at this late stage of the game?

The department had trained me well in the fields of officer survival and self defense. They supplied me with a small, private arsenal-two automatic hand guns each with 16 rounds, a shotgun, an armor plated vest, a car with a radio, should I ever need assistance, a partner to guard my back.

Not a single one of these safeguards or any of my martial arts training could prevent this news from piercing my heart. The hurt had proved to be an expert marksman-the pain had found its target.

At the first hint of dawn I left for the city morgue. The drive downtown yielded more questions then answers. How could I identify the body of a man I hadn't seen in over a decade? Was there no one else close to him who could make the ID. with the ME?

Pushing the thick metal door open, my eyes were instantly drawn to the remains lying on the Coroners' table. The body wrapped in a thick, white plastic bag; the standard heavy duty black zipper to secure its contents.

The cold and lifeless room mirrored the feelings of my heart. The Plexiglas partition between us served as a most reminiscent reminder of our life-long barrier.

The Medical Examiner handed me the wallet that was found on the body. The victims last name matched mine. The wrinkled picture faintly suited my nightmares. His eyes were blue, I had his nose. My signature ended the identification process. Never again would I see my father, at least while I was awake.

The Bhagavad Gita warns us that "for one who has conquered the mind, the mind is the best of friends, but for one who fails to do so, the mind will be the greatest enemy."

For the next four months, my thoughts were far from being my friends. Continuing to blame myself-just as I had done the night I was advised of my fathers suicide-the mental interrogation dragged on.

"What the hell were you thinking?" I inquired of the figure in the mirror. "If only you had been nicer, more understanding, more compassionate. If only you had been a better son." Chronologically I had aged though time had taught me little.

The quiet times were the worst. The department shrink knew better, the local priest new better, my family and friends knew better. Still it didn't matter to me. No amount of counseling or coaching could erase the blame and guilt I felt. The perceived culpability etched indelibly in my heart.

If I believed things couldn't get any worse in my life, once again I was wrong. I had already proven that alcoholism could be hereditary, how about suicide? Every little boy dreams of growing up "to be just like Dad."

The gravel beds spread for miles on the city limits. Midst the mountains of crushed stone and rock hid abandoned vehicles of every sort. It was more re mindful of a graveyard than a junkyard. One could escape into this labyrinth never to be found.

Many an evening found me with my handgun in my lap, noticing how easy it would have been to end the constant head and stomach aches. On the coldest of nights, the stainless steel barrel would glue itself to the moisture on the inside of my bottom lip.

The grooved lines of the gun's front sight acted as a file against my two front teeth. With the hammer already cocked, the slightest pull of my right index finger could do the trick. The Scotch sure wasn't working anymore.

There seemed to be only one way to escape the pain. For six continuous days I thought tonight's the night. Each evening, too fearful to see it through to the end.

Frankly, it wasn't valor or bravery in the face of uncertainty that kept me from pulling the trigger, far from it. Cowardice and the fear of how I would be perceived, postmortem, kept me from taking a bullet. What would my family think? How would the press portray me? Certainly, this is going to look bad. I still hadn't matured. My self image, subject to a democracy, apparently dependent upon the views of others more so than I knew.

The call came in while I was on the four to twelve shift. Dispatch announced over the radio, "Unit 2518- any Unit in the vicinity of Causeway Avenue and the Topshire Town Homes, complaint prepare to copy".

"2518," I responded.

"Unit 2518, any unit in the vicinity, man with a gun complaint. Be advised, the suspect is barricaded in his home and is threatening to kill himself. All units, clear channel one for Unit 2518 and all responding units."

I reached to the center of the dashboard and depressed the emergency red lights and siren buttons. I flicked the switch labeled "Wig-Wags" to activate the alternating headlights.

"Unit 2518, see the complainant, Mrs. Bower. We're still attempting to identify your backup."

"2518 copy, en route," I replied.

All at once fate had delivered me an out. Finally,

maybe things would go my way. It seemed to me that being killed in the line of duty was infinitely more attractive than suicide. There would be a Gold Badge, a nice ceremony for my family including a folded flag and a 21 gun salute. The powerful write-up in the papers would read, "Officer slain in the line of duty." Things were definitely looking up. The coward's way out was starting to materialize.

Lt. Matthews was in the area and offered to respond as a backup. I needed to get to the house before he did. He was a great cop with years of experience. If he arrived first he would surely secure the area and call for the S.W.A.T. Team, and I would definitely miss my chance. As you know, Special Weapons and Tactics has a habit of stealing the show.

As I punched the gas pedal to the floor, the sound of the engine kicking in partially covered the Lt.'s request for me to "Standby and remain down the street from the residence until the other units arrived." Dispatch radioed me to confirm that I had received his orders.

"Control to Unit 2518. Do you copy the Lieutenant?"

Ignoring them both, seconds later I arrived on scene. I pulled over two houses down from the suspect's house and quietly shut the door of my car so as to avoid detection. After all, this was my plan and I didn't need any surprises.

When I got to the front door, the wife and daughter ran out into the yard. I quickly grabbed the child under my left arm and the mother by the wrist, leading them away from the suspects view and field of fire.

"Where is your husband," I quickly inquired.

"Please don't hurt my husband, he's a good man. I don't know what's come over him."

"No one is going to hurt your husband. Does he have a gun with him?"

"Yes, it's a shot gun we bought him for Christmas," she cried.

"Do you know if it is loaded?" She began to scream in panic. Shaking her by the arm again I asked in a slower, more purposeful manner. "Mrs. Bower, do you know if your husband's gun is loaded?"

"A box of shells-buck shot I think-came with it." Hugging her daughter she continued, "Please don't hurt him. He normally doesn't drink this much. He just lost his job today, he's feeling really down."

"Maam, what's your husbands' name?"

"Trent", her answer stumbling over her tears, "Trent Bower."

"Everything is going to be OK," I promised. "Wait here."

The front screen door was ajar and easy to push open with the barrel of my handgun. Calling out to the suspect, I quickly peeked around the corner in an attempt to locate him.

"Mr. Bower, are you in here sir? I'm a cop, don't shoot." Jumping into the front hall I heard him call out to me.

"Come on in, I'm in the living room." I identified myself and asked about his shotgun, there was no response. The situation seemed perfect, there was definitely going to be a shooting, the headaches would soon be over.

I pointed my 9mm around the corner allowing it to lead me into the living room. The suspect was sitting on the couch, cross legged with the shotgun laying across his lap, his head tilted back and resting against the rear wall.

"Hey Trent," I called. He slowly dropped his chin towards his chest.

"Where's my wife and kid?" he asked.

As I looked into Trents' bloodshot, tear-swollen eyes, my heart stopped. There was so much pain, anger and frustration in his gaze. Loneliness and discontent will do that to you. I wondered if my father had cried, how long had he contemplated death, and had it really stopped the nagging pain?

"She's outside, Trent" I whispered. "They're waiting on you."

"You know, they deserve a lot better than me." He paused as the tears began to streak down his face.

"Maybe her parents were right when they warned her I was no good. They'll be much better off without me."

I recognized his frustration with failure-the sick feeling in my stomach and the racing breath; an emptiness of unimaginable depth, where the thoughts of worthlessness and disgust echo each day and night.

Not once did we break eye contact, my reflection in the mirror and me. With this my senses blurred and the room began to dissolve into a whirlpool. It was as if my body had melted into the floor and every inch of the room was now a part of me. His heart beating in my chest. We were two bodies sharing the same soul. I couldn't bring myself to point my gun at him.

"Trent, think about yourself and what you're doing. Take a deep breath, let's not panic, com'on guy. Do you really believe this is going to solve a damn thing? What about your wife and beautiful daughter? How are they going to cope with being left alone. How will they deal with the feeling of responsibility?"

"Why should they feel the blame, its my fault, not theirs." Trent responded.

"Don't do this to them," I pushed. "Your family loves you. They told me so. Deep down you have to know that I telling the truth."

"The last thing I want to do is hurt them." he continued, "They mean the world to me."

"Trent, com'on guy, breath, think about it." The words acted in a self-fulfilling prophecy. My thoughts were of my family and friends. Was it fair to torture my mom the way my dad had tormented me? Would a gun battle erase what had happened? Is suicide really the answer?

As he pushed the shotgun off his lap and on to the couch next to him, both our eyes filled with tears: an instant commonalty of pain. Reaching for the butt of his shotgun, I holstered my own.

"What do'ya say Trent, Let's go see your daughter."

Mark Twain put forth an interesting thought in his literary piece, *What is Man?* He offers "the chance reading of a book or of a paragraph in a newspaper, can start a man on a new track and make him renounce his old associations and seek new ones that are in sympathy with his new ideal; and the result for that man can be an entire change of his way of life." The following morning I would stumble across such a paragraph.

The front of the inspirational card quoted the Danish philosopher Soren Kierkigarrd. "I must find a truth that is true for me...an idea for which I could live or die." My mind was instantly drawn to the urgency of the verse. Why must one find a belief or a conviction on which to build his or her life? Could it be that the absence of such a feeling or "truth", is a prerequisite step towards the feelings of uselessness and shame?

When you open a cupboard and find an empty cracker box or go to the refrigerator and grab a plastic gallon jug that has been drained of its milk or cider, what do we do? Is there much use for a balloon void of air or a pen that has run out of ink? Empty of its contents, the container is discarded.

My thoughts were of Trent from the night before. The greater his emptiness grew, the easier it became to throw away the package. I wondered if my Dad had felt empty and *discontent* with his contents. It was painfully obvious that my life was on its way to the dumps.

Each of us can either summon the means with which to call ourselves out of bed in the morning, or run the risk of lying down forever. To have a purpose is to add substance to your life. To stand for a truth is to append life's value. To refuse residence on the garbage heap is to passionately grab hold of *Something To Believe In.*

CHAPTER II

The Call

•

Not I, not anyone else,
can travel that road for you.
You must travel it yourself.

—WALT WHITMAN

冃

History tells us that the last words of Henry David Thoreau were, "I leave this world without a regret." Can any of us truly greet death remorseless and without sorrow? When life's clock tolls our midnight curfew for the last time, will you and I have any regrets?

As the surveillance of the drug suspects' house dragged on into late afternoon, the brilliant sunset magnified ten-fold as it reflected off the hood of my unmarked car. The crisp orange yellow hue presented the sun as if it were setting just on the outskirts of my view.

Suddenly, a whirlwind of colors and sounds transformed the vinyl bucket seat of my patrol car into a time machine that catapulted me to a distant future. In just a few seconds, I had aged sixty some years. I found myself sitting in a rocking chair, with weathered skin and drooping posture. My shoulders slightly rounded, and the strength in my hands now only a fraction of what I could recall.

With the last rays of the sun dancing across the fields in front of me, the shadows of a distant tree began to stroke my feet. It seemed that fate had granted me the briefest of opportunities to see into my future.

Was I to "leave this world without a regret?" The answer was no. There was, however, a way to prevent this destiny and guarantee that my final days would be guilt free. As is often the case, I had choices and in this twilight they were made clear to me. There were only two options, each as simple as they were direct.

As quickly as age had beset me, the call on the radio snapped me back, my neck jerking forward from the headrest.

"Control to Unit 2518," the transmission sounded.

"Unit 2518, go ahead."

"2518, what's your status?"

"I'll be 10-7 (out of service) on a follow up investigation."

"Control copies 2518. Disregard."

My decision came quickly. The road that lay ahead of me would be a lonely one. My search for Something To Believe In would be a solo case-a one man investigation. No gun, no badge and-worst of all-no partner. For the first time in ten years, there would be no backup responding to this call. From that point on, I would "go it alone."

All that remained was the paperwork. My resignation

would be effective in two days. This final appearance in court, would be my last official duty.

The preliminary meeting with the District Attorney went as planned. We reviewed the evidence in the case and discussed my testimony. We were confident in a conviction and ready for the trial. Walking down the long marble hallway leading to the courtroom, the assistant District Attorney stopped me and asked, "Is it true? Are you really calling it quits?" All I could do was nod my head.

"You know Brian," he paused. "When I was a little boy, all I ever wanted to be was a cop. Hoping one day to have all that power, I would daydream and play quick draw in front of the mirror, red lights and sirens blasting! Giving the orders and telling people what to do. I often dreamt of arresting the bullies of the neighborhood and carting them off to jail." His physical mannerisms matching the excitement in his voice.

My childhood flashed before me. I too had dreamed of such power. Many a day had been spent drawing my gun shaped fingers and hand, pretending to shoot the bad guy.

"Brian, how can you quit? You're leaving the dream. I'll tell you something. If I could have passed the physical, I would have gladly taken the badge over the law degree."

"Pardon," I asked with a questioning tone.

"The only reason I went to law school and later became a prosecutor was because I failed that damned physical agility test." Shaking his head he asked, "How can you give up all that power? How can you just walk away?"

His question haunted me all day; his voice echoing in my mind. He was right. The power was tremendous-an addiction that was hard to beat. What was I thinking? How would I handle the vacuum created by this void of power? How could I surrender control?

When you cannot control yourself-more specifically your thoughts-the first thing you search for is the chance to control others. Whether you subjugate another to your personal demands and whims or to the implied rules and regulations of the state, the law enforcement profession is the ultimate vehicle for control. The doubt began to build within me.

The thirty minute drive back to the station yielded no answers. Neither the faces of the passing motorists nor the voices on the radio offered any clues. It was time for roll call. I radioed control, "2518 to control."

"2518 go ahead."

"2518 is 10-7 for good." I set the microphone on the dashboard for the last time. Unlocking the shotgun, for the first time in nearly a decade, I stepped out of the unmarked patrol car as a civilian.

Lieutenant Matthews was waiting for me in the division room. His only question being the same I had wrestled with all afternoon.

"How can you leave this all behind, Brian?" Pausing for a second, the answer hit me like a bullet. For the first time that day, I had a heartfelt answer.

"If your courage pins on your shirt or rides on your

hip, you're missing the mark. True power doesn't come from controlling other people. True power will only be achieved by controlling myself."

No more excuses, no more crutches. My shield had lasted long enough. Unclipping my badge, I surrendered my weapon-butt first-and said farewell. The echoing voices of doubt were finally stilled. Saluting the Lieutenant, I turned away.

Later that evening, as I stood in line to pay my dinner check, the fortune cookie contained the words of the Taoist philosopher Lao-Tse. "They who conquer others are strong. They who conquer themselves are mighty."

I was a long way from "mighty" and the journey that lay ahead would be a difficult one.

Chapter III

The Journey

•

*The efforts we make to escape from our
destiny only serve to lead us into it.*

—Ralph Waldo Emerson

困

Without my gun and badge I was in a tough spot. I had made too many enemies throughout my career. Survival in New York became more difficult with each passing parole. There were too many who wanted to get even; too many ready to settle the score.

My two door Subaru held everything I owned. You can pack a car so tightly that the weighted trunk rides slightly above the rear wheels.

The road atlas highlighted Chicago, Lincoln Nebraska, Las Vegas then Los Angeles. The beacon of the setting sun was my constant goal. Three weeks and some two thousand miles later, I had gone as far as possible. Venice Beach and the Pacific Ocean effectively blocked any additional advance. To further increase the distance between the Boardwalk and New York, one would have to swim.

As humans, we develop routines quickly that soon

progress to near unbreakable habitude. The ego begins to identify with the commonplace and placates itself with the norm.

For nearly a decade, I had grown accustomed to giving orders and calling the shots: Law Enforcement was all I had ever known. Military and civilian police procedures were my only formal education.

Now the only arrest I could make would be that of my own ego: to handcuff my own arrogance. The sentence was humility and subjugation. Survival meant replacing my badge with a dining room attendant's uniform. My patrol area reduced to the banquet halls of the Los Angeles Hyatt at the airport, the only services to provide were fresh buttered rolls and hot coffee. "Can I clear that plate for you Ma'am?" replacing "You have the right to remain silent."

Like the Police Department, there was a well-established chain of command though now I occupied the bottom rung. My desk replaced by a light gray plastic bus tub. The polyester bow tie grew more constricting with each reflecting memory of my past.

Be forewarned-you that aspire to hold the rose of self control-for it sprouts many thorns.

My badge was more of a shield than I could have ever guessed. My self image had been painted with water colors; the blue of the uniform, the silver of the badge, the red of the flashing lights.

The years in uniform had helped to create an edifice that was leaning towards collapse. No different-I suppose- from a water painting left out in a rainstorm. My defenses could not withstand mother nature and soon began to run.

Los Angeles-the facade capital of the world. Make believe at its finest. What a perfect place for me to hide. All sincerity is counterfeit. All truth feigned. Fairy tales are the cash crop.

My home-at least for the time being-had become the acting crowd. I bussed tables during the day and played make-believe at night. The cable TV movie, my standup comedy on Santa Monica Blvd. The bright lights and cameras posed no threat, microscopes they were not. The various masks held everything intact, the voices of pain drowned by the noise of constant pretending.

Try as we may, there is no escape from the unobserved reality. Each new face, each assumed mask added weight to a foundation already built on sand. Eventually, I would have to pay the price.

Pretending that alcohol did not affect me, I lost my job. Acting like I did not have the responsibility of a monthly payment, the bank took my car. Faking like health was not an issue, I had not eaten in a week. Supposing that it did not matter, I teetered on the edge of Santa Monica Pier.

The call of the wide, dark sea was nearly irresistible. I wondered about the ocean floor; the forgiving qualities of the crashing waves. Would the distant, interior sounds of a sea shell be enough to drowned out the voices of guilt and shame?

Suddenly, off in the distance, there blazed an intense

white light. A mesmerizing beam warmed my face and held my attention. A voice called out to me.

"This is the Los Angeles County Sheriff's Department, step away from the edge."

Lost in a focused gaze, I had not realized that the patrol boat had pulled up beneath me.

"Sir," the voice on the bullhorn warned, "the pier closes at sundown. Leave or face arrest."

As I moved back from the ledge, I could hear the voice of one of the boats' occupants speaking to his partner.

"I think we have a jumper here."

Hearing these words-equally as powerful as the seven rams' horns trumpeted outside the walls of Jericho-all of my pretension collapsed. Monkeys see, monkeys do. Like father, like son. My journey had taught me nothing.

I was still a phony, still not willing to stop the act. I had replaced the gun and badge with the camera and the bright lights of Hollywood. After traveling all these miles, I still could not escape the allure of forcing my own death. My suicidal thoughts were still with me, only buried just beneath the bullshit. The only achievement since New York had been the six months worth of added miles on my odometer. I still hadn't progressed at all.

The following morning's alarm clock was the ring of the telephone. The tearful voice on the other end had sad news. My grandfather had passed away during the night. The funeral would be in two days; my ticket was at the airport.

The cross country flight was a tortuous one. My grandfather means the world to me, and now he too is gone. I felt even more alone.

The funeral homes largest room was packed. Dozens of well-wishers remembering my Pop. Both sides of the main aisle were lined with symmetrical rows of seats; each row a half a dozen chairs deep.

Entering, I first noticed my mother and sister at the front of the room, kneeling side by side. Escalating stages of magnificent flowers encircled the casket. I stumbled into a seat just inside the door.

A half an hour had passed and I still hadn't made it to the front of the room. I sat silently and watched the people file past the coffin. From where I was, it seemed like an empty box.

My mom motioned for me to join her, but I couldn't move my legs. The shaking prevented me from moving a muscle. As long as I stayed seated, I didn't have to see my Pop lying there. I was still able to believe that his death was just a bad dream from which I would soon awake. As my mom started towards me, she once again gestured for me to join her.

"Brian, please," she lipped as she lifted her folded hands to her tear streaked face.

"I can't," I whispered-the sobbing had taken control.

"Please." She met me half way, held me and guided me to kneel. My nightmare was now a reality. I had never known such emptiness. The sound of the loneliest flute pays this feeling no justice.

As the preacher commenced the service with the nod

of his head, I joined my family in the front row.

'If only I were somewhere else,' the Reverend continued with the poem from Noel McKinnis, 'I know my life would be much better there. My prayer was answered. The place was new but my life was just the same....'

My thoughts were of all the places I had run to and of all the situations I had run from. The words of the poem were no longer discernible to me as I drifted off to my youth and back to the lessons my grandfather had taught me. If ever there were a role model, Jack Blydenburgh was it.

The preacher continued, "I've stopped all my running from place to place, from job to job, from person to person. I knew where to find what I was looking for the day I accepted the fact that everywhere I go, there I am." He paused, "This was Jack's favorite poem."

Listening to this verse, I couldn't help feeling that Pop was still trying to show me the way; he was still leaving me clues.

CHAPTER IV

The Dragon

•

We are healed of a suffering only by
experiencing it to the full.

—MARCEL PROUST

困

The drive from the memorial service seemed unusually long-the minutes lasting into hours. "Was Pop really gone?" Like a bone chilling cold, the frigid pain of reality filled me. It would be this truth that siphoned my heart.

Seeing my Pop lying in the coffin unlocked a handful of visions and voices from my distant childhood. Reciting the Greek alphabet before I could read. Trips to the basement on Scudder Avenue to masquerade in his W.W.II uniforms. Pancake breakfasts-after church-at the local V.F.W., Rotary luncheons, Guy Lombardo at Fire Island, Lawrence Welk on TV. Like links in a precisely constructed chain, these memories led to one not so very pleasant.

Viewing my grandfather-lying there with his hands folded neatly on his chest-reminded me of the Coroner's office. His peaceful look and tightly packed lips no different than my dad's. Pop in his best Sunday suit, my father in a white, opaque plastic bag, showing only his face. My every thought seemed blurred with bitter memories of the past in a psychological, gordian knot.

The years hadn't dulled the high spinning shrill and buzz of the bone saw, busy with an autopsy in the room next door. The slightest inhale of the pungent antiseptic smell penetrated every fiber of my lungs. My feet seemed glued to the cold, ceramic tile floor.

Each time I looked in the mirror I saw my father's lifeless face surrounded by the ring of suffocating, white plastic. Initially, the reflections brought out feelings of sorrow and remorse. I felt bad for what he must have gone through; sorry for what I had done.

At first, his last written words ripped to my very core. His pen had truly been mightier than the sword. Thankfully, time had slowly begun to alter my perceptions.

Slowly, I began to see the real intent of his letter. The true meaning of his final thoughts leaked into my awareness. His ultimate plot had been revealed.

The note was clear and direct. His leap from the roof had been precipitated by my outburst on the phone. His "oldest son had shunned" him. He told his friends that I was, "the cause" of his death.

As the months wore on, the true culprit appeared. Self blame was slowly replaced with hatred for what my father had done to me. My memories grew into a source of violent anger unlike any I had ever known. Even the name Paul infuriated me. Various walls in my apartment held the signature of my fist. Rage had supplanted shame.

All my life my father had been selfish and did exactly what he wanted, when he wished, to whom he pleased. From my earliest memories he had tormented me with his absence and he was determined to do the same in his death.

Time had taught me a valuable lesson. I would no longer accept his blame or his condemnation. Only he was responsible for what he had done. Like a victim confronting their attacker in the courtroom, I needed my father to know just how I felt.

All the therapeutic suggestions of screaming at an empty chair and writing letters-only later to ignite them in the kitchen sink-seemed to work well in the moment, though they offered no lasting medication from the pain. The sounds of yelling and crying drowned out the voices for only so long. There remained one final journey; one place I still needed to go.

The anniversary of my father's suicide was in its third year. I had never before visited the cemetery where he was buried. The six hour drive allowed me plenty of time to rehearse, to grit my teeth and clench my fists. My anger was obvious in the reflection of the rear view mirror.

Traveling did nothing to siphon off my interior rage. "Exit 41, here it is."

As the highway sign announced the off ramp, my fury was damn near crippling. Shaking, I asked the toll attendant for directions.

As you pull into the cul-de-sac, an entrance sign above the cemetery gates clearly prohibits the use of motor vehicles. The final approach would be on foot.

Parking the car there was a sudden realization that the tremendous pull-which had drawn me nearly four hundred miles-now had the opposite effect. Something was pushing me away-as if two negatively charged magnets were suddenly joined. The anger that I professed in the car had now turned to fear. I could barely move towards the gate.

The humidity imprisoned the motionless air. According to the plot map, I still had a ways to go. With each forward step my tempo increased slightly.

It was late in the afternoon when I reached the third hill. The shadows of the individual tombstones falling like precisely placed dominos. Their horizontal train directed me to the top of the fourth summit. According to the ground's keeper it was "the marker just to the right of the tree."

Facing west, the name on the gravestone was pinpointed by the rays of the retreating sun. My last name etched in granite; traced by the fingers of my right hand. A numb tingling started first at the base of my skull, down the back of my arms then capturing my wrists and hands. My stomach urged me to kneel.

Tight jawed I growled, "How could you...you selfish bastard?" Instantly-unlike all those hours in front of all empty chair-I felt as if my message was getting through.

"I hate you, with every damned ounce of breath in me-with every fiber-I hate you for what you did to me." Striking my fists against the stone I continued.

"You have no idea how many nights I cried myself to sleep as a little boy, even faking injuries hoping that maybe you would come to visit me in the hospital." Squeezing the top of the marker between my thumbs and fingers in a choking fashion, I continued.

"Most kids wish for Santa Claus at Christmas. All I wanted was a dad."

The setting sun did little to dissipate the heat; the anger flared from deep within me venting from every pore. Still screaming, I stood, repeatedly kicking the grave marker. If he couldn't hear me, he sure as hell was going to feel me.

"Thank God you're not here right now, I'd kill you myself. That's right, I swear I would. You abandoned me in childhood and then in life. If you didn't want a family, why the hell did you start one. If you were going to leave, why didn't you stay gone?"

My assault on the rock solid tombstone did little but cut my hands. My fists couldn't be clenched any tighter, an evil growl replaced my voice.

"I didn't want your damn phone call or your half cocked attempt at a Yuletide reconciliation. Lucky for you you're not here right now. I'd show you pain." Dizzy and almost out of breath I fell back to the ground.

"You may think you've won, that I blame myself for your death, but you're wrong. Where ever you are now, you know it, and you're where you deserve to be."

My itchy, tear swollen eyes pulled heavy on their lids. My fists-just recently employed to punch and strike-now served to rub the salty gossamer runnings of my eyes and nose. My bloody knuckles adorned my face with a natural war paint. I had made my peace. The pain and rage began to subside. Reading his name from the marker I declared, "Paul Alfred Brawdy, we're even."

As I leaned back against the tree, the rhythmic beat of the owls' cry served as a eulogy for all that had been accomplished that day and with each chanting chorus my chin nodded closer to my chest.

PART
2

THE INQUIRY

CHAPTER V

Then There Was Me

•

People generally think that it is the world,
the environment, external relationships,
which stand in one's way, in the way of one's
good fortune....And at bottom it is always
we ourselves that stand in our own way.

—SOREN KIERKEGAARD

困

Awakened by the cool dampness of the late night air, I found myself-my rolled shirt for a pillow-propped against the large trunk of the hemlock tree, that immediately neighbored my father's resting place.

The ebb and flow of the ground mist-covering the cemetery in a thick vaporous blanket-enveloped my legs with only the toes of my shoes visible; each tombstone's shadow engulfed by the thick haze; a most formidable challenge for the best of lighthouses or fog horns. The tangible radiance of the full moon, drawn to the fog with a cadence and pulsation difficult to describe though easy to comprehend.

How long had I been asleep? I must have been out a

while. As I wondered about the time, a sudden whisper startled me and I jumped to my feet. The knee deep fog rushed to capture my sitting space.

"Why are you so hopeless my friend? Do you so long for death that you slumber at her door? Your appointment with the Grim Reaper so pressing that you sit beneath the immediate sweep of his scythe?"

Was it the wind whispering or could it be the hoot of a distant owl or my mind trying to make sense of the cricket's chorus? Wiping my eyes, I tried to place the vague whisper. Squinting with my ears, I first thought, my grandfather's, then possibly my dad's voice? Neither sounding quite the match. The dimly re-cognizable utterance continued.

"This bed that you have fashioned for yourself is inhabited by the living only during the day. At night, the voices come to be the sole occupants of this place."

Still startled I ask, "Who owns this murmur that wheezes from the vapors?"

Immediately to my left, I think I saw a faint glow slowly loft from the ground fog: its dim florescence highlighted by the brilliance of the full moon. The murmur continued.

"To label or tag me will serve you little. Is my advice and counsel any less, while bathed in the obscure light of anonymity? Know that we were introduced when you were very young. Early in life-responding to different calls-we went our separate ways."

I was too puzzled to speak. The voice continued.

"If still you require a title, think hard and set yourself

to the task of re-cognition. Either way you need not fear me and might you choose to embrace me, all the better."

Though I couldn't quite place it, deep inside this whisper was faintly familiar; a tonality I just couldn't quite place. For now at least, its identity seemed unimportant. In such an uneasy setting, its reassuring tone was welcome.

Again it inquired, *"What brings you to such a grave yard? Cocksure, it is not yet your time. Surely you command the strength to pass this cup and fly from death's arrow."*

"My strength to flee need not be questioned. I've been running most of my life."

"From what do you flee?" What has driven you to this end? The soft breath questioned.

"From the greatest adversary ever fashioned by God. An enemy whose pursuit is relentless and who finds me at noon's brilliance or during the pitch-black darkness of a moon less night. Wherever I venture, its voice finds and taunts me."

"Truth be told, I have heard of such a foe," the timid whisper continuing in a sympathetic tone, *"the opponent not easily defeated. Do not despair! Many have learned to prevail and in the end are victorious."*

"Yeah, right." I snapped. "What ever. Since my father's death, everyone has become an expert in my life. The priest thinks he knows, the psychiatrist is sure she is correct, my friends tell me to, "get on with my life"; everyone has an opinion. How could anyone possibly know of the battle I'm fighting or the distances I've traveled to find peace?"

"There is not a living being free from the testing of adversity or the challenge of tribulation. History's burden has been shouldered by many. Why are you so special? Take comfort that you are not the first to have embarked on such a journey-to have crawled about in the dismal labyrinth."

For the first time I began to wonder, "Maybe I wasn't in this alone." Others-quite possibly-have battled before me, some perhaps successfully. Perhaps my struggle was what made me human; my battle a precondition of birth.

With a sound reminiscent of a sudden blast of thunder, the exigent voice commanded, *"No more tears. Do as nature has done, forget the past. The days gone bye are through. By abandoning that which you think you know and so cultivating your enduring spirit, you too shall be successful. Trade your alleged knowledge for the bewilderment of a child. Attend to the silence. Treasure the present. Embrace that which is offered here."*

The only thoughts I could cultivate were those of hate and anger. If I had hopes of embracing anything, it would be my father's neck in my hands. Time was no friend of mine; for it had healed no wounds. Or had it?

Prior to arriving at the cemetery my main goal had been revenge. If the grave was a link or a porthole to the afterlife, I would use it to take one last shot at my dad. He needed to know how I felt.

"Enough is enough." My thoughts interrupted by the murmur.

"Your business is not with the dead but with the living.

No person, no place, no thing has any control other than that which you afford it. Am I to suppose that you truly believe that your father-or anyone else for that matter-is ultimately responsible for where you are in this moment? You speak of the 'search for truth' yet you look afar. Enough with the pointing of fingers and the labeling of blame. If you must know the truth, you must know yourself. Close your eyes in order to see. Attend to the silence. Treasure the present. If you will not grasp it within, you will not grasp it at all. Embrace that which is offered here."

I found myself agreeing with it. My position had been established the day I hung up on him. I said my piece. If he hadn't heard me while he was alive, he wasn't going to hear me now.

Standing in the knee-deep fog, I felt a lightness or weightlessness throughout me; as if the heavy burden of shouldering anger and revenge had been lifted. My rage had been replaced by wonder.

I stood motionless and without words. No longer subject to its yoke, a feeling of vacuity-unlike any I had ever known-began to surface. Had the venting of my fury graveside really worked? My anger was no more. Though in its absence, a vacuum had formed; a hollow, vacant abyss.

There was a feeling of transparency, as if my insides were gone. It became impossible to tell just where the ground mist ended and Brian began.

From the deepest part of my void came the lightning bolt. My *Modus Operandi* had been revealed.

The trip to the cemetery was successful, though not for the reasons initially supposed. I hadn't come to my father's grave to mourn his loss-I barely knew him. My reasons were even more personal and self-serving.

The illumination of the full moon had served to pinpoint my fury. With the help of the shadows, I *re-cognized* the true source of my wrath.

The rage and indignation-here-to-fore directed at my father-was identified for that which it truly was. I had traveled all this way not to mourn a family loss but to grieve the passing of my life long target; the varied excuses for the mediocrity of my life.

My crutches were gone. No longer did I have someone else to blame for my sorrow and pain. All of my life I had a reason for the tears and apathy that engulfed me. What ever ailed me was "my father's fault". He was to blame for what I had become.

I wasn't a professional athlete because my father never took the time to workout with me. I never went to college because he never read me a bedtime story or pushed me to study.

I never made anything of myself because he was never there to be proud of me.

If my father's dependency on alcohol helped him get through the day, so too had my dependency on excuses help me get through my early life. Maybe crutches are hereditary. Along with the blue eyes and whimsical temperament, I also inherited the need to hide behind the blame. Pointing the finger kept the thorough spotlight at arms length.

The oxidizing effect of my excuses had been stripped away. Like an iron fence once covered in rust and now sanded down to its original metal, I felt bare and alone.

Then there was me. I had been exposed; the facade stripped away; my customary pretenses vanished. I was playing a role and the roll had ended. No longer could I adopt this "excuse" or that "reason" as to why my life was where it was.

No more badge, no more acting, no more scapegoats. I-not anyone else-was directly responsible for my current lot. It was time to begin anew, time to cover the bare metal of my soul.

Listening, I realized that the whisper had disappeared. I was, once again, alone and my thoughts were of my dad.

Suicide-the act of intentional self destruction-is but one way to free ourselves from the imprisonment of a masquerading life. Posing so long in our fictitious costume, we soon begin to "loose sight of who we truly are." Even more so than the cliché, eventually we grow deaf to the authentic voice we brought with us at birth.

In-authenticity breeds separation; and the detachment is contagious. Having lost the original connections with ourselves, we soon loose the feelings of association with the world around us.

The feeling of alienation causes us to search for other ways to "fit in." A new mate, a new car, more money and definitely more toys. The list is never ending. The more we search, the sadder we become.

SOMETHING TO BELIEVE IN

Busying ourselves with the constant additions to our mask, we fail to comprehend our heart's departure. You feel depreciated and cheapened. You begin to interrogate yourself. "Is this all there is to life? There's got to be more than this. There just has to be." At this point, the mourning and sorrow are in full bloom.

Inevitably-while contemplating the true value of life-the absence of your chest's pulsation literally "scares you to death." Spiritually, you're done; now all that remains is the biological surrender.

I wondered about those of us searching for peace of mind, though not quite ready to sacrifice life to obtain it. There must be a way to combat the feelings of detachment and worthlessness, without paying the ultimate price.

Pacing back and forth, my thoughts were interrupted by the returning soft breath.

"Life is worthless until the participant in the dance acknowledges his or her call to greatness. Did you not battle with your own thoughts of worthlessness and then suicide. Was it not your desire to extend your boundaries and challenge a cause, that saved you from destruction? Was it not a mission to fulfill that gave you back your worthwhile passion for life? To be alive is to be challenged. Make no mistake. To be great is to simply be."

The tears pooling in my eyes were my only response. Each time I had knocked on death's door, there was something that had called me back. A thought, an urge-maybe a whisper-that interrupted the two stage mechanical sound of a cocking handgun. As the cylinder begins to turn and advances the bullet between the barrel and the firing pin, the sound is unforgettable.

What had prevented me from pulling the trigger? Perhaps a voice that voted "no", a whisper calling for reason, an urging to hold out for just one more moment.

Was it the absence of this authentic voice that allowed my father to jump? Did he call out to the long forgotten voice, only to have it ignore him? Had anger, apathy and alcohol served to arrest the only vote of dissent in his debate between life vs. suicide?

When-in review of his lot-had he found his life too "worthless"? Had the contrived excuses of his life been too thick a wall for the whisper to penetrate?

I thought of the spot at the cemetery entrance where I had parked my car earlier in the day. Through a crack in the thick asphalt, a tiny blade of grass had sprung in an attempt to grow and extend its boundaries. As timid and weak as this little green projectile seemed, its natural potentiality forced it to break through the infinitely heavier cover. In its goal towards *inlightenment,* it would not be deterred.

Now if one were to pluck the blade of grass and use it in a sword like fashion to cut at the asphalt, what would be the result? It is only when the tiny life form is employed in unison with its native potential, that it is successful in freeing itself from prison. It doesn't offer excuses. It doesn't attempt to conform to the wishes of another or blame the cemetery owner for turning its home into a parking lot. It relies on its own voice, its own direction to chart its course. In its desire to be embraced by the sun, no manacle will be too great. The positive whisper concurred.

"Humans are not robots nor computerized automatons, programmed to perform a set task, to run a determined course. Rather an ever budding flower, growing, expanding and re-cognizing the inherent tendencies that lie dormant within, anxiously awaiting re-inlightenment by the Sun.

The only correct path to embark upon is the one that you identify for yourself, the one that viscerally concurs. The rhythm of the beating heart encodes wisdom's cipher.

Where lies the benefit received while capitulating to the dictatorial commands of Chatterdom? Why busy yourself with the pen-always ready to copy some distant text-when only the incision of the scalpel will aid you in your search?

So sad...so sad to see you groping for the candle while in the darkness of another's opinion. The symbiotic allure of Chatterdom leads you down a wide path. Ignore its cry. Close your eyes if you must see. If you will not find it within, you will never find it. Contrary to your core, there is no truth."

As I listened to the growing intensity of the whisper, my thoughts were of a pamphlet I had recently read.

"Believe nothing on the faith of traditions" offered the Buddha, "even though they have been held in honor for many generations. Do not believe a thing because many speak of it. Do not believe on the faith of the sages of the past. Do not believe what you have imagined, persuading yourself that a god inspires you. Believe nothing on the sole authority of your masters or priests. After examination, believe what you yourself have tested and found to be reasonable, and conform your conduct thereto."

This particular teaching of the Enlightened One seemed similar to the training I had received at the police academy. From day one of "Cop School", the recruits are taught to always question that which appears before them. Who?, What?, Where?, When?, Why? and How? are the first questions a responding officer must have answered in order to complete the initial, investigative report. When called to the scene of a crime, the careful unearthing of these particulars may lead to the apprehension of a suspect and ultimately to a conviction.

In my search for *Something to Believe In*—the attempt to gain a worthwhile "conviction" in my life—the application of these investigative tools was but the first step. Self examination—better yet self interrogation—would yield the only clues in this case. The investigation had finally begun.

CHAPTER VI

Big Bang vs. Big Breath

•

Science without religion is lame,
religion without science is blind.

—ALBERT EINSTEIN

困

Once again, I sat with the base of the tree as my cushion and support. Vibrating from within its hollow chamber-I could hear the faint rumblings of some unknown creature as it ricocheted about just beneath the bark of its cocoon.

From my immediate view, only the trees and I sat taller the uppermost layer of fog.

There is a certain medicinal quality inherent in a thick blanket of low level clouds. All of one's senses seem to begin and end right at the tip of one's nose. Slowly-though surely-the muffling fog dampens the advances of the outside world, its humming hush turning my perceptions inward; the reminiscent haze flowed through me or perhaps I through it. Each inhale a testimonial to the quantity of fog, immediately palpable as the quality of its individually minute particulates, traveling from nostril to lung.

Like the rolling drone inside the headphones just before the music begins-or the distant buzz one recollects with their index fingers plugged into their ears-the heavy ground mist acted like a stethoscope as the ebb and flow of my breath scruffed from within.

Just as the newborn mist had inherited its qualities from the warm evening air-coupled with the cool dampness of the cemetery's grasslands-so too had I inherited certain qualities and traits from my parents. Acorns don't fall far from the tree.

If through birth, one acquires various innate attributes and congenital birthmarks, this "passing on" of family qualities and features must be generations old. Surely this consignment of peculiarities is as aged as humankind itself.

My father modeled his father, who modeled his grandfather etcetera, etcetera, all the way back to Adam. My mother's great, great-to the tenth degree-great grandmother was none other than Eve herself. The search of any family tree, yields a common ground or earth in which the tiny sapling was originally conceived. Every member of the lineage contains a bit of the original soil.

Without warning, the security blanket of fog was pierced by a chorus of violent screams and screeches unlike anything I had ever witnessed. The cries-as if two furious cats were engaged in mortal combat-filled the air at an ear piercing decibel. The thick venial ivy-stretched about the mausoleums and marker tops-rattled in accord. Even the ominous, low level clouds seemed to retreat in fear of the ruckus.

Turning in the direction of the brawl, a faint cobblestone path appeared beneath the newly transparent mist. All but my immediate course was obscured by the zigzag design of the many grave markers and stackable tombs.

Working my way through the grave maze-ever focused on the dwindling stretch between myself and the uproarious combatants-my advance was abruptly blocked by a thick of shrubs and dense timber.

The moon's brilliant rays offered no help on the forest floor. Traipsing and treading through the thicket, I eventually stumbled into a tiny opening and for the first time could identify the source of the mammoth tumult.

On the distant side of the clearing, lay two paths slashing a V shape into the forest floor. At the base of the fork grew a magnificent tree. Her far reaching branches-thick and sturdy-were station to an enormous bird of prey; her tremendous wing span creating the sound of a tornado as she flapped and screeched at her opponent.

With one leg attached to the limb of the great tree, she used her free leg-adorned with three massive talons-to swipe furiously at the infidel challenger.

To the right of the screeching bird vaulted a great mound of earth and rock. Atop the pinnacle stood a colossal primate; its massive, pillar like legs solidly grounded to the boulder from which it seemed to draw its strength.

The muscular, well defined primate screamed and

leaped towards the great bird; its sharp, scalpel like nails gouging tremendous pieces of feather and flesh with each penetrating strike.   Sullied and bleeding, the valiant bird breathed on, refusing to surrender. Each warrior headstrong in defense of its territory-in protection of its stock.

How was I to continue on? There was no way to retrace my steps. The fog had erased my retreat. Advancing was my only option.

There I stood-motionless-surveying my possible escape route. Each path-though well trodden-came dangerously close to the powerful grip of the battling titans. My freedom, not to be gained down a popular avenue.

Suddenly, on the ground before me, alighted a small bird; obviously as perplexed as I with the surrounding scene. She paced back and forth, up and down; her actions personifying my very thoughts. Our common goal was escape and survival.

Without warning, the tiny flying creature-possibly a dove or maybe a finch, I couldn't tell-darted into the middle path between the trees' trunk and the base of the great boulder.

Evidently, the bird of prey would not descend from its lofty perch nor would the magnificent primate decline or stoop from its mountain of ground. My friend had fled unharmed.

This would be my only chance. I would need to summon my greatest speed. Sprinting for the razor thin space between the two foes, I escaped to the safety of the primordial forest, leaving the battle behind me.

Making my way through the thick woodland, I eventually stumbled upon yet another partial clearing-the dense foliage blanketed by a somewhat familiar mist. Pausing to feel my whereabouts, I was startled by the friendly voice that had been my companion prior.

Turning to my left, the whisper called to me from inside the canopy of mist and fog. There between us stood my father's tombstone. The combat-still fresh in my mind-pressed to be told.

"I have recently escaped a battle of two tremendous foes..."

"You may be present though you've yet to escape", the whisper interrupted. "Oh, would that your clouded mind shed its useless thoughts, as the snake surrenders its dead skin. Staring too long at the hollow shell, you miss its true nature. The 'battle' you run from is but a reflection on the surface waters of your soul."

"Surface waters?", I questioned.

"The self is hidden far beneath one's surface" the pressing tutor offered. "The hopeful-upon initiating the recovery of deep understanding-are immediately confronted with the ad bivium dilemma; a split or fork in their road to inlightenment.

Misdirected, compelled sightlessly to choose between the 'sacred' or the 'secular'. One willful way leads to a garden originally tended by a curious couple. The other track, to a distant, age old swamp.

The leaders of each direction-confidently sure they guard the 'true' path-see no gray area. The 'Fork' quickly becomes a 'T'. Much the same as two ships diverging from a common course; each mutually opposed to the other.

"One-protected by the image of the cross-heading to greet the new day. The other-beneath the icon of the microscope-sailing into the west. Would the aspirant gaze upon the written word or the petri dish? Any written prayer or noted postulate is of no use to you.

My mind wandered back to the morning that followed my father's suicide. As clear as day I saw myself reading the desk blotter marked "1987". In the upper right-hand corner, scribbled in blue-black ink was the name "Father Tom." The phone number of the church was familiar to me. Written in the opposite corner of the desktop calendar was the name and number of the department shrink.

The first to call was the priest; he would keep me in his prayers and suggested that I "surrender to God's will."

Hanging up one line to take another incoming call, it was the psychiatrist offering "therapy and-if need be-medication."

Both confident in their own solutions; neither willing to incorporate the other. From the outset, it was obvious that they both meant well and maybe I was more to blame for the tug-of-war then they were. Perhaps their contrasting polarities existed only in my mind.

"From what demented soil springs your contradiction between science and religion? What confused, misdirected thought squanders and muddles away the incalculable benevolence of time by pondering its homeland as either brain or mind?" The requisitioning voice

demanding to be informed.

"What benefit to you to welcome this battle in heaven? What malady summons the cherubs from their assigned post?"

Shrugging my shoulders was my only response.

"Like a pair of scissors with only a single handle, one is useless without the other. Thankfully, when death arrives to retrieve her mask, they will know each other; only then will the facade be dissolved. The End erases all pretense.

Let the ageless battle of either/or be fought by the cohorts of Nietzsche and Kierkegaard. Though a legacy, it is surely not yours.

The investigations of science have uncovered our original Mother while the religious contemplation of the sages heralds the arrival Our Father. The union of the two offers us the loving care of both parents.

Not unlike two Cyclops battling for a clear view of the truth, only when they embrace each other-shoulder to shoulder-is their vision focused on that which is real. See, with both eyes closed, that which is offered here. You have two ears to listen, so hear."

The debate over the polarities wrestled for my attention with my head weaving here and there.

Suppose, that in the perennial debate of Religion vs. Science, you tend to side with the Evolutionists and the theories of Mr. Darwin, and in doing so you choose to travel the secular route as opposed to the sacred. The genesis of innate creativity is even more powerful.

Presume that our initial spark of life originated with the Big Bang. An exploding cosmic fire ball sent the universe on its course. As she began to grow and expand, various suns, planets and moons were created. Some time down the cosmological road of production, humankind was developed an spawned. Based on that humble beginning, we were eventually composed.

Without the discretion or instruction of an outside deity, life as we understand it, was brought to be. Life created itself. Even in the jungles of Africa only the "strongest survive." It is those strengthened in the skill of creativity that continually withstand the attacks of their piers. Our basic instinct is to create and thus survive.

I listened intently as the voice began.

"Take the advice of the wise Hippolytus and 'abandon the search for God and Creation and similar things of that kind. Instead, take yourself as the starting place. Ask who it is with in you who makes everything your own saying, 'my mind', 'my heart', 'my God', ('my science'). Learn the sources of love, joy, hate and desire. If you carefully examine all these things, you will find God in yourself'".

From the early days of Sunday school, I can recall the first lines of the Bible in Genesis. "In the beginning God created the heavens and earth..." Save chaos, there was nothing before him. In the lineage of humankind, God was first. The deity is the base of the family tree.

Now with genealogy in mind, is it not fair to assume

that if God is our great, great, great grandfather, then do not we also possess some of his qualities and character traits? If he is the starting point of the human lineage, does it not follow that he must have contributed in some way to the contents of the DNA that we possess today?

Most religions-in one terminology or another-believe that we as human beings were created in the image of the primordial deity. Does this mean that God thought it would be a good idea to model us similar to his image so he graced us with eyes, limbs and a heart? Is our pedigree highlighted solely by the physical body, or is there more?

God was a manufacturer by trade. He was the original composer, the first architect, the primordial inventor, the pioneering artist. That was his calling. He chose to create. He was an artist. One may even look to the occupation of his son, Jesus for leads. Jesus, just like his father Joseph, was a carpenter.

He in an attempt to keep the family business going, he opted to follow in his father's/Father's footsteps. He was a carpenter, a builder, an architect, a creator.

Suppose that this is our gift; that humankind inherited from God an artist's touch. When God created us "in his image", he gave us the ability to see things that did not yet exist-not just simply a pair of eyes. Imagine He presented us with the ability to hum tunes yet to be composed-not just simply a set of ears.

Presume that our ability to transport ourselves to unknown, distant lands, has nothing to do with our legs. We travel because our minds have the artistic ability to take us there.

The essence of humankind is truly reflected in her ability to create. As an artist you may paint, sing, raise a family or even write. The world is full of artists that never get published, never have their work hang in a gallery or played on the radio. Expressing your inner passion, your true talents; this is indeed life's ultimate art form. To surrender the creativity of a child is to banish oneself to hell.

So here we are. At the base of our family tree lies common ground. Science or Religion. The Big Bang versus the Big Breath. God as Father or the Universe as our Progenitor. Either way, the one quality that lies dormant at the core of all humanity is its will to create; to bring forth into this world that which has here-to-fore existed only in our minds.

It is this natural call to artistry that suffuses our lives. That whisper that propels you forward has but one goal-the desire to create anew. Confronted by the challenges of life, it is your potentiality and ability to compose a creative solution that is your most fundamental inheritance form the original deity. To be human is to be an artist. To breathe is to pace the Avant-Garde.

As humans, we are driven, better yet compelled to constantly attempt to construct the life we desire, even if the tools we choose are injurious to our well-being. My father chose to create the life he wanted with the aid of the bottle. Sadly there are many today who attempt to paint their world with drugs. I spent my early years sculpting excuses in a misguided attempt to formulate the existence I desired.

Even our "bad habits" were originally adopted in an attempt to formulate the pain-free, happy life of our dreams. Our habits-good or not so good-were all originally adopted with the best of intentions; to make ourselves feel whole. When dis-content, we search for ways to fill the void.

Regardless of our station in life, we have created the platform on which we stand. The opaqueness that obscures our vision is self-constructed. To focus on anything, other than our *inlightenment,* is to miss the mark. My thoughts segued the whisper.

"Why not let the pundits, the scholars, the masters of alleged knowledge battle over their monocular schools of thought. The convoluted halls of Chatterdom are home to many an orator. Why waste your inherent potentialities in the frivolous, perennial debates of the Big Bang versus the Big Breath? One big ego over the other. The dispute serves only to agitate the waters and thus obscures their true reflection.

Be it the natural evolution of an exploding fire ball, or a heavenly breath respired into the dust which bid our birth, the commonalty is in fact the parental ground. Debate as they may, the technique or method of the original birth, the progenitor is one in the same.

Search the ultimate origin of the Family Tree for your true nature and power. All offspring receive certain traits and qualities as payment for accepting the role of birth, so too were you given the powers of Father Time and Mother Earth. Your will to create runs long and deep. Actively employ your heredity. Acorns fall close to the tree."

Chapter VII

Nature

•

My soul can find no staircase to heaven
unless it can be through
Earth's loveliness.

—Michelangelo

闲

While pursuing the essence or the basic underlying quality of an object or person, we usually inquire as to their "true nature".

Might one decide to further investigate the original essence of the word "nature", he or she will soon discover the Latin word "*natur*".

Suppose we take our search one step further, by searching any dictionary with an etymology section, the relationship between the word "nature" and "natal" is unquestionable.

The roots of nature and birth share a common ground. As sure as our "biological parents" are responsible for our birth at the micro level, our great (to the tenth degree) great, grandmother is Mother Nature herself.

As my thoughts came back to the present, the friendly whisper called for my attention.

"Too little you discern in nature that is yours. Focus on the ambiance of your environment, let her be your teacher. The Book of Life contains four chapters, winter is but the first of these. Interrogate the seasons with the essays attached. Instruct them to direct you. The sole answer you search for abides in the marrow of her jurisdiction. All you will ever need is found in the trees and the streams that bring them water."

The thick blanket of fog seemed to transport me like the moving walkway at O'Hare International; the magic conveyer belt of mist routed me through the maze of marble and trees.

The moon's light edified all the inhabitants of the canopy as it perched above carpet of ground fog. Every tree borne creature of the night, busy scurrying from limb to limb-the multiple fingered branches stretched and suffused into the near night sky as if its very arteries and veins. The circulating corpuscles of sap pulsating in rhythm with the stirring breeze.

Interrupting the nocturnal chorus, the wise whisper offered, *"Investigate nature in search of your answers. If you must question outside of yourself, interrogate the rushing brook, the map on the back of a newborn leaf, the sharpness of a blade of grass or the direct statement of the crickets. Strewn everywhere are the creations to be modeled and re-viewed. Is it not through the paternity of the bird that the airplane soars?"*

My attention-momentarily drawn to the sound of a distant running creek-was recaptured by the focusing admonishment of the passionate little voice.

"Why so intrigued with the various celestial comets of the evening heavens, yet the origins of a passing thought interests you not? Do not go abroad. Return home. That which is artificial soon offends the palate.

In your midst sleeps the passion of a moving glacier and the power of a tropical storm. Do not content yourself with egotistical thoughts and fancies in an attempt to identify this inner realm. Abandon all that you pretend to know and surrender your weakest sense, for your eyes will betray you.

Hear, feel, embrace and nurture the power that suffuses your body. Just as the earth's nucleus contains an explosive core, so too are you centered around a fiery and passionate heart.

Her reserves of oil and gas are surely no different than the inner fuels that ignite your true essence and power your innate will. Her diamonds, her silver and gold are but the sparkle and gleam of a child's inherent voice prior to the application of the institutionalized anesthetics of the mob, the herd, the gang, the clique, the cult.

There is no truth more original than this: as the off-spring of nature and the direct descendants of the planet, you too enjoy and command a vast reservoir of natural resources. Everything in nature contains all of her strength and power. To be alive is to breathe. To breathe is to command a Herculean potency. Do not ignore your inheritance. Re-cognize that which is offered here."

I wondered out loud, "How does one tap into this reservoir? How can I begin to retrieve my share of the power?"

The answer to my own question came quickly. The voice was clear and direct.

"Like the erupting volcano or the shifting plates of the earth's surface, you too will find a way to release your core energy. This potential will lie dormant and docile for only so long. Your will to create cannot be ignored. Who but you will head these words?

The earth does not care what plans humankind has for the release of her natural potential. She will erupt and shake, steam and crack, submerge and rise as she deems fit. So too will the wise ignore the constructed labyrinths and Procrustean plans that society has laid for the release of their true potential.

Creativity without authenticity is simple conformity, and conformity is the arrow through the heart of the artist within. Many will model the centrifugal force of the cesspool in their search. Set YOUR sights on the whirlpool if inlightenment be your goal. To live is to breath and create anew. Shut your eyes, hear your heart beat. Only then will you know."

A roaring clap of distant thunder punctuated the moment. Ominous clouds-highlighted by the backlight of the moon-began to build on the near horizon; the leaves now rustling their advanced warning. Duets of thunder claps and lightning bolts danced across the agitated sky.

We continued onward in retreat of the storm.

CHAPTER VIII

Self Reliance

•

It is your own assent to yourself,
and the constant voice of your own reason,
and not of others, that should make you believe.

—PASCAL

The sole concern of learning
is to seek one's original heart.

—MENCIUS

困

As we ventured away from the storm, with each step the whisper grew increasingly tangible. The weak, feeble light that I had first met, now reminded me more of a brilliant roman candle or phosphorus roadside flare. Glowing with a confidence that was invigorating and certain, the longer we conversed, the more confident I grew. Like spending time with an old friend, I felt comfortable and embraced.

As we walked, my thoughts were of a childhood Sunday school lesson and the story of David and Goliath. The young champion, standing on the opposite hill top and viewing the nine foot tall philistine warrior-decked in a bronze helmet, protected by a two hundred pound coat of mail, armed with a sharpened bronze javelin and matching shield-still was not shaken in his courage. The giant combatant roared,

"Do you need a whole army to settle this? I defy the armies of Israel. Send a man who will fight with me".

This continued for forty days, morning and night with none brave enough to accept the challenge.

The first book of Samuel tells us that young David witnessed Goliath's challenge and accepted forthwith. Hearing this, David's oldest brother labeled him a "cocky brat" and a "ridiculous little boy" and told him to go home.

David confidently replied, "When I am taking care of my father's sheep, and a lion or a bear comes and grabs a lamb from the flock, I go after it and take the lamb from its mouth. If it turns on me, I catch it by the jaw and club it to death. I have done this to both lions and bears, and I'll do it to the Philistine too."

The Young David possessed an unshakable self-confidence that would not be deterred. The army commanders outfitted him with a coat of armor, a lance, a shield and sword and after donning them, David refused saying,

"I can hardly move!"

Reaching down he picked up five smooth stones from a nearby stream and loaded them into his fanny pack. Replacing the soldiers' sword with his sling and the infantryman's lance with his shepherds staff he ran out to confront the great Goliath.

Words were exchanged and the battle commenced. David-using only what he had known as a child-loaded his sling with one of the pebbles and hurled it at the mighty giant, striking him in the forehead. Goliath fell to the ground and was defeated.

How would the battle be remembered if the young David listened to the opinions of those around him? What would the outcome have been if David had taken the advice of the "experts" and clothed himself in the "proper attire?" Would history have remained the same if the "truths" of young David's contemporaries had served to eviscerated his soul?

How many times have you been told you're "too young"-or for that matter too old- "too inexperienced" or too "x" to achieve your goal? How often have you armed yourself with the heavy, awkward rumblings of the herd? How many times have you surrendered your beliefs in an attempt to gain admission into the clique?

The "tried and true" has many advocates. Thankfully, Truth is not determined by popularity.

Had David been persuaded to ignore his intuition and abandon his sling and pebbles, he most certainly would have lost his battle with Goliath. The young David was victorious because he relied on himself and that which he knew to be true.

Pausing to check my relationship to the advancing storm, the whisper stayed the sounds of the crickets and of a distant owl.

"It is as the Bhagavad Gita suggests, 'Better thine own work is, though done with fault, than doing others' work, even excellently. They shall not fall in sin who fronts the task set them by nature's hand.'"

"Sadly", the heavy-hearted whisper continued, *"You forfeit a majority of your power under the guise of conformity and acquiescence. By sacrificing your position and surrendering to the thoughts and wishes of the cackling crowd, you expel yourself from heaven and thusly cast into the bowels of hell. None save you, can see the clarifying measures of the epiphany. Pace the paceless. Appropriate that which inheres. Ignore all but your own intuition"*

"But what of those whom act as guides, as seers, as gurus?"

The response of my companion was instant.

"Why must you mimic the poor, frantic moth, darting back and forth so near to an open flame. Flying too close to the fiery words and beliefs of another will surely melt your resolve. Has the lesson of Icarus taught you nothing? Search your root, hear the words of the wise Cicero, 'Nobody gives you wiser advice than yourself.'"

The short pause composed a deafening silence. Not even the wind dared to stir.

The imperative voice continued.

"Remember always that you are the way, the path, and the light. It is a familiar voice that hails to you from within the Whispering Oak of Dodona, of this you can be sure. There is but one guardian angel, yet you search afar. Opaqueness gains strength in distance. Close your

eyes." As the voice progressed, its cautioning tone rang evident.

"Be advised, do not misread the invitation of Socrates to 'Know thyself' as a static benediction; seen as such only seeds a fruitless path. Behold his counsel and recognize the thought as the precursor to its dynamic twin, Direct Thyself. Only then will the sown seed blossom.

Be your own guru and worry not over the proper education. Manifest the Christ that is your midpoint. Be your own Buddha, let your own Tao shine forth. There is but one expert from whom you would seek council. Brian, mind the chord vibrating deep.

Though it casts many sparks, truth is but one light. To be inlightened is to be in the dark. To learn is to forget. To be wise is to be a child. Transcend intelligence, leap into the light of bewilderment. Those who long for action, are trapped by the deep fog, yet the deepest, thickest fog awaits those in pursuit of knowledge. Attend to the silence. Treasure the present. Embrace that which is offered here."

Nearly spellbound by the wise words of the whisper, I had lost track of the approaching storm that had settled directly overhead.

In an instant, the swollen clouds let loose their burden. It was as if the sudden shower had come forth to wash away my ignorance, each little droplet as a chisel on my facade. My mask was not waterproof.

The "truth" that is true for anyone is that which affords them a drill and rig to tap into their *natural resources.* We possess all the raw materials we need to ignite our true passion. The only correct path is the one traversed and fueled with this native energy. You can mine your own resources and annex your own assets. There are no experts save the one in the mirror.

I remembered the whisper.

"Trusting in oneself is a contagion that springs deep from the core. There is but one 'genie' in the bottle of your facade. Once it is summoned it is difficult to repress. The potentiality is Yours alone. Who but you knows this to be true?

Why not ignore the sense driven babble, cackle and clatter echoing throughout the labyrinthine, cockroach infested halls of the ant heap entitled Chatterdom?

The ranting, woeful bricklayers of these catacombs seeks to embalm you. They have constructed your prison with the baked clay of conjecture and with the blasphemous mortar espoused from their puny, pedastalled soapbox. Ignore this extroverted trowel of dung. They offer you no direction; their path into the shadows.

Pace the paceless. It is your own ears that block the truth as a window shudder blocks the adopting rays of first dawn.

Attend to the silence. Appropriate that which inheres. Embrace and cherish that which is offered here."

Chapter IX

The Faces of Evil

•

"There is only one good-knowledge,
and one evil-ignorance."

—Socrates

困

The earlier raindrops posed as a simple advertisement for the raging storm above us. The gusting winds had shaken an owl from its home and evicted it from the tree-tops. Things are different here: cemetery trees interpret the conversing winds differently than any other trees known.

We set into a pathless swatch of evergreens, adopting the largest of the magnificent trees as a shelter from the storm. The ground beneath-adorned in a velvet blanket of moss and countless pine needles-served as our porch.

Side by side we sat-entertained by Mother Nature's concert: the tubas of roaring thunder, the clarinets of crackling lightning accompanied by the howling winds and the cymbals of rain against the newly formed puddles.

Just to the left of the lowest tree branch stood a mound of freshly dug earth. No doubt created by the caretaker's shovel, the pile of ground and soil resembled an ancient pyramid; its base obviously wider than its peak.

With little time elapsed, the assault of the tiny raindrops began to take its noticeable toll on the summit of dirt. The relentless pounding of the small globules of eroding water soon had won the battle. The natural sculptor had laid the stockpile to a muddy bog.

"Oh the mighty showers whose diligent attention to detail has returned towering mountains to their original birthplace." The exacting voice continued.

"If only human hearts and minds were as susceptible and pliable to the artistry and purification of these tiny, pharmaceutical solvents. Wickedness hides from no greater fear.

"Even the most deep seated evil and malign plaque lay erodible in the presence of these drops of holy water. Just as it quenches the summer wild fires of the forest, so to it would strangle the burning infernos of hell."

"Do you mean the Devil himself and if so, how is it that these little drops of rain can combat such a mighty foe as he?"

The interrogation began.

"Where sleeps this Evil One, this Satan or Lucifer that you insist?"

Once again my thoughts were of first grade Sunday school at the Methodist church, the lesson of the Fall from grace and the post-baptismal temptation in the desert.

"Was it not the Devil that tempted Adam and Eve into original sin?

"Once again, attend to the silence. Treasure the present. Embrace that which is offered here Brian." The speaker renewed.

"Those who search for evil outside themselves are surely lost. Evil does not thrive naturally. Wickedness is so because it is unnatural: an abomination and perversion of the truth. You have been warned before to 'bring forth what is within you', and if by ignoring this advice 'you do not bring forth what is within you, what you do not bring forth will destroy you.' Evil and Sin are nothing more than two twins that conspire to bind and extinguish your inner light and the potentialities of your foundational will. Evil is that which inhibits your natural kinesis.

Fear, not Satan or the Prince of Darkness lest you view him as a reflection in the pond at your feet. Evil will surely engulf those who fail to be inlightened by that which is offered here."

The apocalyptic voice dispatched a nervous chill throughout my body divesting it from the warm, comfortable feeling it had appreciated just seconds ago. What of all the lessons of childhood and the warnings of those who had gone before us? Could the Devil be a remnant of our ignorant youth?

We all share distant memories of the threatened punishment we would receive if we "misbehaved", or were "naughty" or anything other than "good little girls or boys".

Suppose the idea of the Devil be thrown on the junk heap with the 'boogie man', the 'monster under the bed', the 'phantom' in the dark closet and even the list keeping 'Santa Claus'?

I thought carefully before venturing another question.

"If, as you say my friendly presence-and I surely have no reason nor excuse to doubt you-the figures of Satan, Mephistopheles or Diabolos are all but fabrications and phantoms of the mind, how then does one combat this evil? To where should I turn for lessons on how to slay this fearful dragon?"

The reply was instant.

"Cerberus-Hostis Humani Generis-the guardian of that which is within you, dons three masks: Fear, Ignorance and Boredom.

There is no evil-subjective or otherwise-without the dark combination of these three ills. The aspirant will recognize their threefold relationship if freedom is the ultimate goal."

It seemed to make sense me. If heaven housed a holy trinity, why not a three headed hound to roam the hallways of the hell?

The resolute voice continued.

"The underworld is that realm that lies buried beneath the masquerades and disguises that imprison your soul. Your beast and its domain are your own fabrications."

You point to the actively pacing Cerberus yet lay no plan to escape his grasp. You speak of fear but fear of what? You suggest re-cognizing our ignorance yet offer no clues for scholarship. You warn of boredom yet run in no certain direction. How will I ever learn to combat this foe?"

There was a deafening pause.

"The clarification you seek lies in your heart. The identity of evil, the 'Fibber' is known to all. The 'naked truth' is that which is void of all disguise and masquerade. Carefully review that which is uncovered here.

"The first head of the dragon is that of Fear. Those held in its vicious jaws are frightened by the pangs of rejection and ridicule. They worry about violating the 'shoulds' and 'should not's', the 'coulds' and 'could not's', the 'musts' and 'must nots' of their overly opinionated peers.

Their light is spent in a quest for popularity and normalcy. Doing so, they forever shackle themselves with the fear of public denial and remained imprisoned, strangled by the habitual desires of clattering clique.

"Ignorance, the center head of the beast, is by far the most vicious. Its thunderous growl fills the ears of those who might listen. The call of ones true potential and will to power is drowned by the raucous screaming. The inner spark, constantly yearning to ignite, is ignored in the repetitive din and clatter. Their true potentiality rejected and scrapped, it eventually succumbs to the winds of doubt, the lonely embers slowly suffocated by breathless time.

"The final confrontation is with the grimace of Boredom. Crippled by Fear, powerless without their primordial spark, these victims crawl apathetically towards the grave. The paralyzing unresponsiveness to the call of their own heart, leaves them lethargic and disinterested

in their true potential and native bliss. Look for them on the smooth path or one forged by another, too fearful and ignorant to set their own course. What greater evil can there be?"

As the whisper finished, I began to realize that for one to be saved, there need only be an exorcism of ignorance.

"My useful whisper, the veraciousness of your confessions serve to officiate my every thought. How long will your wisdom stand as the ever alert sentinel at the gates of my reason? Your directives penetrate-as if my earlier confusion were imaginary-the thick rind of murky self reflection; all false perception peeled away."

Fear and boredom seemed to be a by-product of a clouded reality. By *re-cognizing* our innate potential and passionately carving our own path to salvation-with the machete of bliss-we courageously accept the challenges of life. (In an instant Michelangelo's words-"with chisel in hand all is well"-made perfect sense to me.)

It is only when we ignore the whispers of our own reason, that we bind ourselves to a personally created hell ruled by the devils of our choice.

The origin of the word devil is the Greek *diabolos,* that literally means "one who throws something across one's path." Satan-the "adversary" or one who "plots against"- is that entity that blocks or opposes the release of our authentic potentialities.

There is no evil other than that which "plots against" or "throws" an obstacle "across" the path that leads to your Something to Believe In. Like a choking victim, evil blocks the very breath of life.

Viewed in this light, evil is more like an apathy, an inhibition or a negation-conscious or otherwise-of the potentiality that resides, part and parcel, within each and every one of us. Like the fundamental figure that "called out" to Michelangelo-longing to be liberated from the suffocating marble-we too lie deep within a restricting pretense.

This restrictive, smothering stone has been plastered on us since birth. In an attempt to mold us in certain image, to teach us the "correct way", to "protect us from ourselves", to lead us down whatever path the experts in our lives chose to dictate, the facade was introduced.

With the goal of security and the spackle of 'should' and 'should not', 'must' and 'must not' you began the construction of your prison.

I have a distinct childhood recollection of my grand-mother-on my mothers side- and her beloved rose bush-es that bordered the front and sides of her home. Each fall she covered her prize flowers with a large Styrofoam cone so as to protect both buds and thorns.

New York winters, with her frigid temperatures, heavy snow and pelting ice storms-were no friend of my grandmothers cherished possessions. Slipping, sliding and falling rooftop snow would spell sure death for the roses if not for the security of the protective cones.

Just for a moment, suppose, that upon the arrival of spring, my grandmother had failed to remove the protec-tive shields. Soon, as the summer developed, the maturing rose bushes-in an attempt to grow and ripen- would commence pushing against the walls and ceilings of their asphyxiating prison. To no avail: the stifling cones had been fastened with the utmost care, well grounded to prevent a stiff wind from dislodging them. Shortly, the beautiful flowers-robbed of their potential to bloom and offer the world their enfolded scent-would slowly begin to die. Never having the opportunity to sing their natural song.

Habitude is a fierce jailer. As children, we were covered with these protective layers and thus remanded to our cells in the name of "what's best for us."

Unfortunately, many today-enslaved by habit and complacency-seldom attempt to remove their Styrofoam cones. That which initially protected us now sets about to destroy us.

Perversion is the end result of over protection, and the lack of desire to molt that which no longer serves us. We surrender our potential and conform to the internal shape of the old, smothering cone. We relinquish our birthright and succumb to an existence highlighted by what Henry David Thoreau labeled "quiet desperation", and his foreboding words still shackle us today:

The youth gets together the materials to build a bridge to the moon, or per-chance, a palace or temple on the earth, and at length, in middle age concludes to build a woodshed.

With the bars of apathy we have remanded ourselves to

a formidable "woodshed". The English poet William Wordsworth offered us this:

Our birth is but a sleep and a forgetting; The soul that roses with us. our life's star, Hath had elsewhere its setting, And cometh from afar: Not in entire forgetfulness, And not in utter nakedness, But trailing clouds of glory so we come From God, who is our home: Heaven lies about us in our infancy! Shades of the prison-house begin to close Upon the growing boy (child).

Wordsworth's "prison-house" is self constructed. Satan is not bound because he is Satan. He is Satan because he is bound. Capitulation and submission have dulled our intellect and left us spiritually impotent. The opaque facade leaves us-like the "Prince of Darkness"-blocked from the light.

Creativity and inner passion have been traded for the "pleasing shapes" of conformity and alleged security. Many have never abandoned the childhood drawing game of "connect the dots". In adulthood, we remain content to live "between the lines" and allow someone else to number our dots and manacle our creativity. Life is surrendered and the death march follows the sequential path of 1 to 2, 2 to 3, 3 to 4, ad infinitum. Stumbling, submissively forward, our habit acts as quicksand drawing us ever nearer to death.

Inlightenment does not consist of traveling to a distant place in hopes of discovering a buried treasure, nor does it demand mimicking the mantras and mannerisms of an alleged "expert". There are no maps, or steps or blueprints. The buried treasure lies dormant just beneath your chest, anxiously awaiting your personal summons.

The fading storm offered signs of retreat and once again there was a quick glimpse of the moon.

Chapter X

The Rainbow's End

•

Nothing is so certain as that the evils
of idleness can be shaken off
by hard work.

—Seneca

Knowledge without experience is
worse than useless.

—Common Aphorism

囷

In seeking harbor from the storm, I had not realized that
we had descended a small embankment. As I stepped
from beneath the sanctuary of the evergreen limb, the
earliest hints of dawn began to overtake the brilliance of
the full moon; tiny fingers of sunlight grabbing up the
deep shadows of the past.

Climbing the rain slicked hill, I paused for a brief
moment on a level plain-all the cemetery spread out
before us-the entrance gate still a ways off in the distance. The night seemed to have slipped away. The nine

hours looked more like twenty minutes. I was anxious to start for home.

"My thoughtful whisper, your message is clear to me. The cocoon must be *broken before the butterfly is free: the young Tadpole can not leap. Inlightenment is action, evil is apathy.* Even so, I must make certain to occupy the direct and proper path before venturing further. To struggle and toil down an alternate, indirect path, only in the end to find my labors misapplied, this indeed would *bestow the sorrows of the fool.*"

My memory was full of the varied odysseys and miscellaneous, mis-taken paths of my early life. Hoping the gun and badge would bring me power, turning to alcohol in search for clues. With each acquisition, the cavernous void at my core grew ever larger. In a mis-directed mind, two embellishments in the bush are worth one assurance in the hand.

Neglecting the Truth that lies dormant within us, creates a gluttonous vacuum. The subsequent pain and loneliness are the parents of a ferocious-never sleeping-cavity. The lost ones forage about, attempting to feed the empty space at home.

The "demons" thrive on the echoes of this void: the spiritual equivalent to the stomach growl. Your appetite grows ever insatiable and the misdirected patronage of these cravings leaves you in contrast with your authentic self. Ever growing dis-content with your contents.

I have long believed that Adam and Eve were banished from the Garden of Eden because they longed for something outside of themselves. God did not evict and punish them over a piece of fruit. They were exiled from themselves when-compelled by discontent-they journeyed outside of themselves in order to gain contentment: reaching for the apple to satiate their hunger.

No doubt, a promise as tempting and enchanting as the double flute of the Sirens. As Circe warns Odysseus:

The imprudent man who draws near them
never returns, for the Sirens, lying in the
flower-strewn fields, will charm him with
sweet song; though around them the bodies
of their victims lie in heaps.

Many have been lured down the wrong path by attending to the flowery advice and enticing suggestions of voices contrary to their intuitive selves. In doing so, they march to the beat and percussion of a luring though misdirected drummer.

The call of a morning bird brought me back to the present.

"Oh friendly spirit, it is as you say. Most of my life has been spent *running in circles; traversing a course set by others.* The years of confusion have left me tired and weak. The song of the *lethargic fool* is sadly familiar to me. Many *lift their feet only after the sand grows too hot to step upon; apathy is a hard course to surrender.* May the true call of my intuition-not the perilous song of the Sirens-spark my gait.

"Freedom from my self-imposed hell will be realized with the *liberation* of my neophyte's soul; all the while overcoming the *inhibitions and societal limitations that have here to fore confined and confused* me. There is but one point on the map of *inlightenment*. Only the blind *frantically search the horizon*. True passage offers no journey. I must till the ground that holds me."

"Thank you for making your deal so clear in my mind. I need but *one tool* to plow this earth and to reap its garden of paradise. If I opt to remain unschooled in its application, forever will I remand myself to the great abyss. Though I wonder where am I to find such a tool and how will I know how to use it?"

"Once again, you're right. My question does indeed contain the answer. It is as direct as that. To breath is to be alive, and to ponder and deliberate the thoughts that present themselves while focused on the dance of inhalation and exhalation, this is my sole task.

"MY hopes of *inlightenment'* too often do drown in the sea of din and clatter. Like the gravitational pull of the sun, the allure of *Chatterdom* is mighty. Who but I- in my natural potency-can resist her pull. For those chosen few—the *strong of heart and breath*—meditation is focused silence, with the *inner wind* as their sole guide.

"To travel in the full embrace and awesome view of nature with an attentive stillness and mindful hush, this will be my meditation.

"Why would I bother with all the varied gymnastic contortions or with the pre-fabricated vocalizing of that which can not be spoken? Why not consciously focus on the sound of my own breath, indeed this is the sole tool I will ever need.

"Your message seems clearer to me with each passing

minute. Through a *playful breath the fundamental self is seen.*"

My thoughts were of a recent phone call. My friend was disappointed because he had spent the last ninety minutes of his day-in preparation for meditating in the company of the setting sun-hiking to the top of a small mountain that bordered his hometown.

By the time he ascended the top, spread out his blanket, stretched his legs and finished preparing to meditate, the sun had just set.

His voice could not hide his frustration.

"I was so disappointed Brian, I really wanted to meditate."

Contrived meditation is a core contradiction, a root oxymoron. To strain, struggle, and toil in hopes of achieving a state of relaxation and poise is to wander in a wasteland; a stumbling subjugation to someone else's "dots".

To commune with nature silently and without expectation is the only worthwhile source of meditation. It is the contemplative reverence and deep respect for the unity of the soul and the powers of nature, that yield true *inlightenment.*

Your breath is the same wind that rustles the mighty treetops and transports the immortal clouds. Some things in life are so basic, yet we seem destined to complicate the simplest of things.

"The avenues in Nature are many oh friendly ghost. *The sacramental call of the sparrow* does indeed *direct me to the face of God.* Only the wise *capture a glimpse of the deity on the bottom side of a maple leaf.*

"Full of benefit are the moments spent watching the passing clouds brush against a mountain range or caressing an urban skyscraper, re-cognizing that it is the play of my breath that fuels them.

"Listening to a crow caw or a neighbors dog speaking, viewing-with awesome wonder-a new found sea shell or the rain drops as they play tag with the earth. All these are one in the same. I will not *lose or abandon the fundamental uniqueness of childhood.* Children are no strangers to the many faces of truth. I will simply *breath and believe.*

"Your arrow hit its mark when you declared that I would not re-acquire my inherent wisdom like some *token or bauble that is lost or misplaced.*

It does indeed lie dormant interiorly, encased in the persuasions of *fear, ignorance and boredom:* my fundamental voice overwhelmed and mired with the 'should haves' and the 'should not haves', the 'must' and 'must nots' propagandized by the chattering mob, the herd, the gang, the clique, the suffocating cult.

"Only I possess the tools and implements necessary to dredge this stifling bog and release my natural resources. Your admonition to use my breath as *the drill* seems absolutely correct.

"Just like a childhood past-time of igniting a square of paper with the focused rays of a magnifying glass, so too can I use the intense focus and concentration of my inner light to burn and *melt away the facade that imprisons my authentic, fundamental self.*

"How true! It is in fact the embellishments and constructions of the indirect mind that choke the aquifer of my vital force. True Light-that fuel tapped during meditation-is the only sword that I possess in the battle with the prince of darkness. I will surely let my oldest companion be my only guide. I can't thank you enough for all that you have offered me!"

Minutes passed in quite reflection, with each thought I gained more courage.

"You're totally right. The world has no room for cowards. The *most masterful of birds confront the stiffest of winds.* You'll see, I will *put straight* my life. The path to destruction does *bend oblique* For the rest of my days I will *close my eyes and enjoin the light directly.* For if I do not *find it within* I *will never find it at all.*"

Suddenly, a dashing beam of random brightness penetrated the voluptuous, slumbering clouds.

Glancing down to shade my eyes, I realized that I was all alone. By facing the sun, the shadows of the past had vanished. The sentence of guilt and shame repealed; my execution stayed.

Gone were the nervous stomach and rapid pulse which had initially accompanied me through the cemetery. In their place, a firm, even bliss; a steady contentedness, neither too much nor too little of any emotion I had ever known; a space with no polarities.

During my journey to confront the memory of my dad, only the first hours were spent in turmoil-the rest in peace.

The cemetery gate stood directly in front of me.

CHAPTER XI

The Pot of Gold

•

> *What if you slept, and what if in your sleep you*
> *dreamed and what if in your dream you went to heaven*
> *and there plucked a strange and beautiful flower, and*
> *what if when you awoke you had the flower in your*
> *hand? Ay, what then?*
>
> —SAMUEL TAYLOR COLERIDGE

困

In the beginning, the rolling hills of tombstones filled all of my rearview mirror; seconds later, only center stage; a half a minute further, they were all but gone. Home, and a nice warm shower, were still a half a day away.

For the first time in months-maybe even years-I felt a tranquil sense of peace and calm. Thankfully, my mind was no longer riddled with guilt and shame. The stress of sadness, blame and contempt-for my father and for myself-no longer haunted me.

As a young boy, I thought I was the cause of my father's rage. Whether he drank, yelled, smacked or even ignored me, somehow I always felt responsible for "making him mad." When he would leave for days at a time I believed it was my fault. When he didn't come home, I was surely to blame. Years before my father took his life, I felt culpable for his absence.

Finally, I was free from the dark cave of reprehensible guilt. As the mythological dragon selfishly guards the fortune of valuable gold and jewels, so too had the memory of my father prevented me from capturing the wealth that was once mine.

The shadow of the dragon had blocked the sun for so long that my native homeland had been rendered a "wasteland." In its dark presence, nothing could grow. Directly confronting my fears had set me free. The kingdom had been saved. The dragon was no more. All that remained was the duty of planting the garden anew.

The solitude of the drive allowed me to focus on the "dream" of my own heart.

"What do I want out of my life? What do I believe in? What am I all about?" By addressing my intuition directly-minus the din and clatter of guilt and stress-I had begun to *re-cognize* its natural voice.

Fastening my concentration on the rhythm of my own breath, one word continued to repeat itself in my mind. Attempting to make sense of the time spent in the cemetery, this one word kept whispering off my lips: *"Direct."*

How had I buried the memories of the past? *"Directly!"* How could I now cultivate my own garden? *"Directly!"* How could I begin to help others re-discover the inherent value of their own lives? *"Directly!"* How must one find their own *Something To Believe In?*

"Directly!"

For the rest of the ride, my mind continued to whisper, *"Direct."* If there was any way to re-enter paradise, the oblique path must be abandoned. The direct approach is the only way to Truth. Inlightenment can only be realized in conjunction with the Truth that resides within us.

In any labyrinth, the only way to freedom is the direct route. Left, right, back, forth, up and down is a sure recipe for confusion and stressful bewilderment. We lose ourselves by adhering to the crooked, indirect, tension filled path.

I wondered how my dad-and others-had found themselves in the middle of an isolating maze; cut off from the world outside of the zig-zaging walls? Their feeling of exasperating loneliness only compounded by a deep rooted sense of detachment. What toll must the pressure, stress and strain of isolation take on the human mind?

I myself had been painfully aware of the feelings of separation from the world around me. As I sat on the Santa Monica Pier, there was a definite attraction to re-unite myself with the deep, dark ocean. Tired of being separated and divorced from the rest of the world, death seemed like a loving, pain alleviating reunion with my old family. My medication seemed to be contained in the waves below. The prescription waiting to be filled by Nature's salty taste.

What was it though that had called me back from the edge? Why hadn't I gone through with it? My father had jumped, why hadn't I? Was it a question of courage-or the lack thereof-or was it a question of common sense? There would be only one way to answer either of these questions.

The entries in my journal that afternoon attempted to decode or clarify the direct meaning behind the whisper. Often times putting a thought down on paper helps to solidify its meaning. This time was no different. I would confront the blank pages of my notebook armed only with my pen. Its design, device and motif would follow directly.

How is it that the saying goes? "The shortest distance between two points is a straight line." A synonym for the word straight is...you guessed it, direct. In your search for *Something To Believe In,* the only true path is the direct one, the straightforward route of your heart.

The worrying masses are those trapped in the dismal ups and downs of the mercurial labyrinth. In my life prior, instead of understanding and relying directly on myself, I was battered about in the maze of outside opinion and habit. My path was not my own.

In my quest for *Something To Believe In,* the search for knowledge finally led me to my-self. That "truth," as Kierkegarrd writes is that which "is true for me, the idea for which I could live or die." This "idea" is simply a belief in your-self: a belief in that Truth that lies at your core; it does now as it always has.

The only true prophecy in your life is that which is self-fulfilling. The only protection in life comes from self-assurance. Your belief, your Truth, is determined by self-analysis and is then self-applied. Self-defence through self-awareness is the only shelter from the storm.

Your goal of *inlightenment* and true independence will become reality only when you become in-dependent on yourself. In order to successfully achieve any goal (Inlightenment included) you will want to rely directly on your-self. There is no one else to blame or applaud, other than yourself. You are the way. You are the light.

To identify that Truth that is true for you, and then apply that Truth directly to the world around you, this is "the only end in life." To be self-centered is to be centered on the Truth that is within you. To be centered on your self and to attend to the commands of your own intuition, this is the only Life there is. You were born to manifest your truth

Now to many, the above suggestion may sound like a recipe for hedonistic, selfishness. That is simply not so. By truly and simply (without all the pomp and pretense) understanding the mission of your self's center, this suggestion becomes more palatable. Selfishness is a trait of those who, upon ignoring their hearts call, timidly look outside of themselves for a sense of self worth.

Fearful, mis-directed people lie, steal and cheat in an attempt to ignorantly, (the word I would use to replace the word selfishly) fill the vacuum created by the lack of *self-centeredness.*

Children-and even some adults-"act out" in an attempt to objectively fill the void of the self's center. Temper tantrums for attention, excessive alcohol, drugs, food and sex are all simple attempts to fill the core's whole and to gain a sense of completeness. At the core of the pendulous coward roams a hunger that demands to be satiated.

Think of the analogy of two balloons. The brightly colored, well rounded, consciously high flying balloon represents the individual courageously suffused with their centered belief in themselves. There is no pressure because the interior air is in complete concert with, and in *uni-son* with, the exterior air.

Now those, shriveled, darkened, grounded, deflated balloons represent those who have chosen to remain (temporarily I hope) ignorant of the truth that lies within them. They sheepishly attempt to obtain fulfillment by taking outside stuff in hopes of inflating themselves.

The memory of their ultimate selves is vague. They are tortured by the twins of "Dis" and "Un": Dis-content, Dis-couraged, Dis-gruntled, Dis-satisfied, Un-happy, Un-healthy, Un-wealthy, Un-wise. In an attempt to self-fulfill they unknowingly (stressfully) hoard all they can get. They do not re-cognize the truth. Inflating the balloon with the full presence of our hearts desire, shatters any confinement that has been constructed to shield or restrain us.

Like a compromised damn that can no longer handle the determined river from flowing to the ocean, breaking through the suffocating ideas of the collective allows you to free your natural resources. It is this emancipation that releases your Truth. Notice how it streams and pushes to manifest itself in the lowlands of your life. Truth and happiness are self-fulfilling.

I often think back to the evening in the cemetery and the suggestion of the whisper, "The body can be a cruel and demanding landlord; the original tenant is easily forgotten." It is this (hopefully temporary) memory loss that keeps you from your homeland.

Seek as you may for outside intervention, the "Genie in the bottle" can only make your dreams come true after it has been emancipated from its glass prison. Up until then it remains impotent and week. In an attempt to ride out the stressful storm of life, we remand ourselves to the air tight bottle for comfort and protection. Many of us are too busy surviving to ever truly live.

In acronym form, the word D.I.R.E.C.T. spells out those actions that guarantee the successful manifestations of your true hopes and beliefs. Thoreau believed that "as is our confidence so is our capacity." By understanding and applying the power of the D.I.R.E.C.T. Acronym, you can begin to increase your confidence and discover your inherent Truth.

By focusing on the "real you" the prison walls begin to weaken, the snare begins to fail. You and you alone are the sole keeper of your jail. *Re-cognize* who you really are, forgive and forget the misgivings of the past. You are the *soul* cause of where you are in the moment.

The next moment depends on you, directly!

PART
3

THE GOLDEN FLEECE

CHAPTER XII

Decision

•

*Each soul achieves its own ultimate success by putting
forth its own best effort effortless. Allow me to tell you
how success is one: Do your own duty,
as seen by your Inward Sun.*

—THE BHAGAVAD GITA

*An aim in life is the only fortune worth finding. It is not
found in some foreign land, but in the heart itself. To be
what we are capable of becoming is the only end in life.*

—ROBERT LOUIS STEVENSON

困

Destiny is not a matter of chance; it is a matter of
choice. It is not a thing to be waited for; it is a thing to
be achieved." So wrote the turn of the century American
orator William Jennings Bryan. Like destiny, your
Something to Believe In will not come about as a matter
of happenstance or chance. When it reappears, it will be
as a result of your decision to actively rediscover its
meaning in your life.

Similar to a fresh lump of clay on the potter's wheel, your dreams, your destiny, your heart's desire, sits within you as untapped potentiality, anxiously longing for actualization. It will not be born through luck, accident or fate. Nor will your potential be manifest in the absence of your personal request. You alone can make the decision to *re-awaken* that passion that lies deep within your center.

You may describe this as a "calling" or your "life's work" or even the awakening of your "true self." Regardless of its title, it is that one thing that calls forth from your intuition. It is the true meaning of your life.

According to Jesus-as quoted in the Gospel of Thomas, "If you bring forth that which is within, what you bring forth will save you. If you do not bring forth that which is within you, what you do not bring forth will destroy you." Adhering to the former, actualizing your true meaning will save you. By *re-cognizing* that which is already within you, your authentic self is saved from the stressful onslaughts of external fabrications and objective embellishments.

"Nothing can bring you peace but yourself", so Emerson tells us in *Self-Reliance*.

"Simply the thing I am Shall make me alive", so offers Shakespeare. To be "saved" is to expose your truth, your dreams, your destiny, that lie deep within you. Plain and simple.

The inverse of this thought is as simple and direct. Pretending to be what I am not-blanketed by a constructed facade-shall facilitate my death. As a butterfly that never escapes the confines and limitations of the caterpillar stage or the tadpole that-never responding to the call of its own heart-remains confined in its murky pond. It is this selective decision to remain in the dark cellar of life that thereby abdicates your right to the throne.

To not bring forth your dreams-to not tap into your natural resources and employ your raw materials in a recipe for *dis-ease*. As Ortega y Gasset preached in his powerful work, the *Revolt of the Masses,* "An unemployed existence is a worse negation of life than death itself."

At birth, we are all "born naturals." We all enter this world as a prodigy, as a genius. As we grow and attempt to conform, it is the negation of our soul, of our hearts' desire that leads us into the black labyrinth.

"In our early youth", the philosopher Arthur Schopenhauer tells us in his *On The Sufferings Of The World,* "we sit before the life that lies ahead of us like children sitting before a curtain in the theatre, in happy and tense anticipation of whatever is going to appear." In our youth, excitement and anticipation are the fuels of our passion.

Henry David Thoreau believed that "the youth gets together their materials to build a bridge to the moon, or per-chance a palace or a temple on the earth, and at length, in middle age concludes to build a woodshed."

As Emerson puts it," So nigh is Grandeur to our dust, so near to God is man, when Duty whispers low, *Thou must,* The youth replies, *I can.*"

So what happened to your youthful "can do attitude?" Where are the "high spirits" you possessed in your youth? Where is your memory of who you truly are? Why have you abandoned your "bridge to the moon?" Perhaps the ancient sage Epictetus can offer us a clue.

"Every habit and faculty" he believed, "is preserved and increased by correspondent actions; as the habit of walking, by walking; of running, by running...After sitting still for ten days, get up and attempt to take a long walk; and you will find how your legs have weakened."

With each new day of age, we grow ever more appeased with the pastime of surviving, all the while ignoring the innate art of living. Instead of pursuing our hearts desire, we plot our daily survival. Our life is weakened with every attempt we make to merely survive.

Your focus is your real-ization. When you focus on survival, you real-ize your existence as a struggle. What you fixate on, you inextricably fasten to your life. The thought you concentrate on converges your imagination with your external reality.

Now, your mind, which can truly only concentrate on one thought at a time, focuses on that which it is most accustomed to. If your habitual thought process focuses on survival, your mind is incapable of identifying the desire of your hearts' dream. Soon-rather proficiently-you remand yourself into the prison of the daily struggle. You banish yourself from your garden of paradise. Circumstance dictates the wins and losses.

Many of us ignore our ability to chart our own course or

carve our own path and only walk on those roads that have been paved for us in advance. Our legs-wrought with atrophy-are weakened because we never run and tumble through the high grass and weeds of the virgin path. Our lives grow interwoven with the need for outside opinion, direction and conformity. Though the seed is cast, it is sadly cultivated by the babbling mob. This is a most troubling stress to the soul.

Subsequently, our inner voice is ignored and inlightenment is sought down the paths and alleyways of those around us. The "road to destruction is broad and the gate is wide" because it must accommodate all those ahead of you yelling back, "hey, follow me".

"I'm so lost, what 'should' I do?" replaces *Sapere Aude!* (Think for Yourself).

We abandon the innate in pursuit of the ornate. We ignore our inner voice and look outside of ourselves instead of relying on that which is near at hand. We content ourselves in the shadows of outside opinion instead of bathing directly in the light ourselves. The abdication of the soul is an age old concern. Centuries ago Aesop warned us of this habit in the story of *The Dog and the Shadow.*

"It so happened that a dog had just received a piece of meat and was carrying it home in his mouth. Now on his way back to his den he had to walk on a small bridge lying across a pond. As he crossed, he looked down and saw his own shadow reflected on the surface of the water below. Believing it was another dog with a better piece of meat, he made up his mind to have the other chunk of meat as well. So he took a snap at the reflection in the water, but as he opened his mouth to grasp at the new piece of meat, his piece fell into the stream and was carried away."

Mencius concurred with Aesop writing, "The path of duty lies in what is near, and individual seeks for it in what is remote". Or as Thomas Carlyle, a contemporary of Emerson wrote, "Our main business is not to see what lies dimly at a distance, but to do what lies clearly at hand."

So many of us "snap" at the distant reflections of today's gangs and cliques, sadly surrendering that which we already possess. Like the Dog in the survival mode, we appease and adorn ourselves with the fabrications and contrivances of those around us.

Seldom content with those things that we already possess, we struggle down the indirect path in search of our "daily bread." Soon stress and tension take a deadly toll. By believing that someone or something else holds that which will make us full again, we search outside of ourselves for sustenance and nourishment. We surrender life, by begging to survive. Our lot is cast to the wind.

Your *Something To Believe In* is here. It lies within you, having never left. Your destiny lies within us-close at hand.

"Great Brian, Its in me. So how do I regain this knowledge?"

All you might do is decide to *re-cognize* that which is

truly ours. You must choose to abandon your mindset of survival and allow your dreams to shine through. YOU must *re-cognize* your "Inward Sun".

"Is re-cognizing it enough?"

"Just trust in yourself" Goethe tells us, "then you will know how to live."

Having yourself as the focus of something to believe in, is the first step. Then, by trusting, and believing in yourself and in the natural resources that you possess, you begin to experience life as it was meant to be.

If "seeing is believing" than doing is knowing. Let's get to it.

The D.I.R.E.C.T Acronym

The first letter of the D.I.R.E.C.T. acronym stands for *Decision*. You responsible for the decision to listen to and trust your intuition-to follow your heart-this is your first step.

What are your dreams? What is your ultimate desire? What course would you set if you were certain you would arrive, if you successes were guaranteed? How best to deploy your raw materials and natural resources will come later. For now, focus on your destination, where you want to be in life.

In attempting any goal, you must first know where it is you want to end up. If you do not identify your destination initially, how will you ever know if you have arrived. Even when your goal is inlightenment, you need to know what it is you are truly searching for. You must create a picture in your mind first, before you set out. Your future litmus test of success begins now.

Throughout my days as a cop, there was no greater asset than my partner. When it came to gathering evidence, interviewing witnesses and hopefully closing cases, the aid of an assistant was paramount.

Since that time I have relied heavily on another partner in my search for *Something To Believe In*. This new found assistant is Nature itself. There is no greater associate.

Suppose, for the moment, you can't quite put your finger on what it is that you ultimately want to do with your life. What if on your first attempt your intuition is inaudible and you decide to coax it a little. How can you place a "direct call" to your hearts desire?

Solvitor ambulundo: it will be resolved walking. By spending time in the womb of Mother Nature, you slowly begin to quiet the mind and recall the inner voice of your heart. There are many distractions in our world today and sometimes it can be difficult to hear your inner voice through all of the din and clatter. So what is the student of intuition to do?

Thoreau gives us a hint when he tells us, "that there is a subtle magnetism in Nature, that, if we unconsciously yield to it, will DIRECT us aright." Additionally, he suggests that "It is the marriage of the soul with Nature that makes the intellect fruitful, that gives birth to imagination."

The next time you are outside-in a mountain range or

in your own back yard-close your eyes, inhale slowly through your nose while filling the bottom of your lungs first, and as you exhale, mimic and focus on the sound of the wind gently blowing through the trees. Continue until you feel the sense of calm pooling up from deep within you.

Inhaling once again, hold your full breath for a few seconds and notice how you can begin to *re-cognize* the faint beating of your heart. Pay attention to the subtle feeling of your heart as it pumps your blood. With time you will be able to hold your breath for longer periods of time, always increasing your focus within.

As you grow more and more capable of hearing your own heart beat, so too will you learn to *re-cognize* the whisper of your own intuition. The gentle whispers of nature will point the way. In the beginning, this is the only meditation you will ever need.

Do not be discouraged by the discursive thoughts and mental ramblings that pop into your mind, and for heaven sakes, regardless of what the "experts" say, do not force those thoughts away! We live in a society that is a quick example of the penalties of ignoring our inner selves.

Listen to the thoughts and then re-focus on the sound of your inhalation and exhalation and notice how they mimic the roar of the ocean shore or the breeze through the trees. Use your natural surroundings as your spouse. Partner with Nature. Stress and tension are human made. Their absence is noticeable in Nature With its help, investigate, interrogate, and discover. Search for clues in all that you see. Focus on your breath. Listen to the sound of your own hearts' pulse. *Re-cognize* the voice of your intuition. Uncover your desire.

If you could spend a day doing anything, and I mean anything, what would you do? Forget about criticism or the fear of being unsuccessful. *"Saper Aude"*.

What dream would you manifest if you knew your success was guaranteed? What fantasy would live in if you could just create it? The great Swiss psychiatrist Carl Jung believed that the debt we owe to fantasy and imagination is "incalculable." Do not forget the similar suggestion of Albert Einstein when he offered that your knowledge is second only to your imagination.

Breath, think and be merry. This course is yours to decide. Your ultimate desire is your destiny. Quiet the mind and listen to the whisper near at hand. Walk in nature or relax on the ground watching the clouds drift by and *re-cognize* your inner voice. It's in there. Listen to it and live. Expressing your inner passion, your True talents; this is indeed Life's ultimate art form.

Carve your own path. Spin your own potters wheel. The decision to either survive or to really live, is yours alone. Hail and cheer those ideas that arouses your heart and fill it with passion. Ignore the "experts" and the direction of the established crowd. Heading the call of *Chatterdom* will only bring you stress and tension. In your life, you call the shots. Isn't it true that you-and you alone-hold the keys to the prison that you helped to create?

CHAPTER XIII

Initiation

•

*If you have built castles in the air your work need not
be lost. That is where they should be. Now build the
Foundations under them.*

—HENRY DAVID THOREAU

*Nothing will content him who is not content
with a little.*

—GREEK PROVERB

困

In the year 1501, the great Michelangelo stood before
an eighteen foot long piece of flawed marble. Now this
particular piece of stone had been lying in the yard of the
local church yard for almost a third of a century. Other
artists had attempted to work with the stone but because
of an imperfection on its surface, it was deemed flawed
and "unacceptable".

How many of us have sat around most of our lives
because someone else said we were flawed or unacceptable? How many times have you let the convictions of

others determine your inherent worth? This assessment did not seem to trouble Michelangelo. He believed that God had placed the figure within the marble and that by removing the excess constrictions, the statue could be liberated from its marble prison.

"The more the marble wastes, the more the statue grows." Michelangelo would also write, "Just as, by taking away...hard and alpine stone, a figure that's alive and that grows larger wherever the stone decreases." How would your life grow if you could decrease the stress and stone like tension that envelopes you?

The powerful artists first duty was to create a *direct* model of the statue that he knew to be trapped within the marble. He fashioned a small replica of the stone's unmanifest potentiality and used it as a guide. A few short years later, Michelangelo unveiled arguably the greatest statue ever released: the fourteen and a half foot figure of the young champion David.

Now, this story is powerful for two reasons. First, because it speaks to the champion that lies within each of us, and that is anxiously awaiting its release. Many of us slowly suffocate within the imprisoning cone. We are "born free, and everywhere (we are) in chains."

Oliver Wendal Holmes agrees with Rousseau. "We are all tattooed in our cradles with the beliefs of our tribe; the record may seem superficial, but it is indelible." What indelible chains are currently keeping you from your *Something To Believe In?*

As you sit beneath your suffocating cone dreaming of a day when you may free yourself from the "chains" and "tattoos" that restrict your true potential-are your thoughts not of an eventual awakening. Your goal is not to "find yourself", but to find a way in which to "arouse yourself".

You have the raw materials and the natural resources you need, of that there is no question. It is not a journey to discover your true potential rather, the decision to expose that which you have always possessed.

"Compared with what we ought to be, we are only half awake. We are making use of only a small part of our physical and mental resources." William James continues In his *Letters,* "Most people live, whether physically, intellectually, or morally, in a very restricted circle of their potential being. They make use of a very small portion of their possible consciousness, and of their soul's resources in general, much like a man who, out of his whole bodily organism, should get into the habit of using and moving only his little finger. Great emergencies and crises show us how much greater our vital resources are than we had supposed."

Years of spiritual conformity and personal neglect have rendered us weak, drained and stressed out. The challenge to re-awaken your true potential and manifest your innate desire is hampered by the forces of apathy and atrophy.

The "emergency" that presents itself now is your call to life. Like the traveling Gulliver who awakens to find himself tied down and imprisoned, so to do we find ourselves tethered and restricted by the tiny thoughts and beliefs of the jibber-jabber gang and of our past experiences of survival. Your desire summons you to act. The decision to live, not just survive, calls you forward. When you re-cognized your "D" you set the ball in motion.

There is however, only one way to re-invigorate and unchain yourself. Emancipation is defined as "the act of setting free". How is it that we can set ourselves free from the sloth and apathy of our lives? How can we loosen the grip of the marble prison?

One chisel at a time, one chain link at a time, one breath at a time you can begin to rescue your true self. Mark Twain offers us this thought about patience and tenacity. "Habit is habit, and not to be flung out the window, but coaxed down the stairs one step at a time."

What steps can you take-right now-to erase the habit of relying on others? How can you "coax" yourself "one step at a time" into the future, all the while ignoring the misdirected rumblings of outside opinion? Once again we can turn to the lessons of a brave, little youngster.

The story of David's rescue from the marble is also of importance in this particular chapter because of the fact that a small "scale model" or plan of action was employed to aid in the emancipation of the imprisoned hero. One chisel, one hammer tap at a time, Michelangelo set out to achieve his goal. With a direct plan in his mind, he meticulously peeled and pared the stone, a single piece at a time. With each fall of the mallet, the champion grew closer to freedom. Each chisel strike moved the artist closer to his heart's desire.

Having initially identified your *Desire,* you now can move to *Initiate* a direct model or plan of action. To free yourself from the marble that traps your natural resources, you need a plan.

The masterful architect Daniel Burnham challenged us to, "Make no little plans; they have no magic to stir (hu)mens , and probably will not be realized. Make big plans; aim high in hope and work, remembering that a noble logical diagram, once recorded, will not die."

A great plan is only as powerful as its inception. Aristotle believed that, "The first step is what counts: First beginnings are the hardest to make and as small and inconspicuous as they are potent in influence, but once they are made, it is easy to add the rest."

There can be no initial step greater than the decision to manifest your destiny; the re-discovering of your true potentiality and natural resources is a noble goal. Deciding to courageously embark on your quest for *Something To Believe In* signified your first step. Your subsequent goal requires the formation of a "logical diagram".

Like any road map that highlights the desired destination-keeping it in constant focus and then identifying the smaller routes that, once combined and totaled, place the traveler in their desired location-you plan will be a clear cut, step by step map.

20 Minute Victories

Let us first return to a fable of Aesop—*The Golden Goose.* "Thinking to get at once all the gold the goose could give, he killed it and opened it only to find nothing."

What do you suppose would have been the outcome if Michelangelo anxiously worked with a jackhammer or Picasso with a can of spray paint? Can you bake an apple pie in a microwave? You might want to turn to the lessons of nature. A snake cannot molt or shed its skin in an instant, it takes weeks for a butterfly to brake free from its cocoon, and obviously an infant requires months of rolling, crawling and stumbling before he/she can walk. Perfection in an endeavor takes time.

"First say to yourself what you would be;" wrote Epictetus, "Then do what you have to do. Practice yourself, for heaven's sake, in little things; and thence proceed to greater."

Having defined your *Destiny,* your next step, is to identify your steps, in the direction of your goal. Say to yourself, "Here I am now. How can I get from here to there"? Listen to the intuitive answers to your own questions and rely directly on yourself. It's time to *Initiate* your game plan.

"What can I learn, right now, for the next 20 minutes, that will move me closer to my goal?"

"In the next 20 minutes, is there a lesson Mother Nature can teach me? Is there a book or conversation I can learn from?"

"What can I do, right now, for the next 20 minutes, to re-awaken my true potential?"

"In the next 20 minutes, how much more of my ultimate ability can I re-gain?"

These answers supply the individual rungs in your ladder. As an individual brick, they seemingly hold little worth, though pieced together, they create a mighty force. One well planned move after another and the goal is *real-ized.*

I have a friend who was born in Ethiopia and he now lives in Chicago. He offers us this old family proverb: "When spider webs unite they can tie up a mighty lion."

As seconds are to hours, it is the aggregation of the little goals that lead to the culmination of the greatest achievements. Without the minute hand there would be no need for calendars, no meaning in time.

In Nietzsche's *Thus Spoke Zarathustra,* he offers us this. "(They)He who would learn to fly one day must first learn to stand and walk and run and climb and dance: one cannot fly into flying."

So let's begin to fly. Grab your journal and a pencil. Allow yourself the next 20 minutes to accomplish this victory.

At the very top of the page, write your desire in bold, inch high letters. Now, drop all the way down to the bottom of the page and place the # 1 on the very last line. Counting from the bottom up, number the lines from 1 to 30 so that your numbers end just below your *Desire.*

Returning to the bottom of the paper, this becomes your first 20 Minute Victory. Once again question yourself. "What can I do, right now, for the next 20 minutes to move me closer to the achievement of my dream"? Write your answer at #1.

You can approach the answer to #2 in one of the following ways.

One, wait until after you have accomplished your first 20 Minute Victory and then question yourself as to your next move or, should you decide to use a more a priori approach-and remember the decision is totally yours-you can imagine that you have already achieved the successful completion of #1 and then immediately answer the question for #2, and so on, all the way up the list.

Either way is sufficient in terms of building your "logical diagram" You may decide to experiment to find out what works best for you. By focusing on the little steps, the 20 Minute Victories, your success grows in a cumulative fashion.

Now in the right-hand column of the page, list your "natural resources", your inherent talents, your "God given abilities."

"Oh but Brian, I don't know what they are. It's been so long." Think back to the last time you were successful in achieving a goal. Interrogate yourself. Investigate your past triumphs. Your natural resources are still with you, you must simply begin to identify and then employ them.

Now, how did you tap into your natural resources the last time you were successful? What tools, traits or talents did you employ? What were your "strong suits?" Be specific! As you begin to list your talents, assign each of them a letter of the alphabet.

OK. Return to the list of 20 Minute Victories. Choose the letter or letters that mark your personal talents and match them up the numbers on the left side of the page. Decide on that trait or traits that you can call upon to help you achieve that particular 20 Minute Victory. Apply this selection process for each of the numbers on the page so that each line has both a number and a letter or letters.

Sit back, take a deep breath, focus on the sound of your own inhale and exhale and begin to study your "logical diagram." Run your plan by your intuition. The end result will amaze you!

In addition to paving the way, your 20 Minute Victories uproot the tangled, intricate origins of procrastination. Be it due to fear, laziness or simple lack of desire, by agreeing to undertake a task for only a third of an hour, you soon realize that your movements are your moods. The small "action-ette" is not as distasteful as you first thought, is it?

By participating in a particular project or task for just twenty minutes, you soon forget the reason for procrastinating in the first place. Have you ever taken a shower in the morning and only washed half of your body? How many times have you only read one word on a page? Most times-in minute 21-the thought of stopping will appear more foreign to you than initiation did in the beginning. Your movements will have changed your mood.

Cultivating the artistry within is a slow, purposeful task. Success does not come overnight nor is your true potential manifest instantaneously. If you wish to advance into the infinite, explore the finite in all directions.

"If the Infinite you would stride, pace the Finite's every side." Goethe continues, "Whatever you can do or dream you can do, begin it. Boldness has genius, power and magic in it. The present action that springs from within sets your proper course."

You might begin your initiative into your infinite potential by "exploring the finite" that lays in front of you like cobblestones on the road of your destiny.

As St. Augustine suggested, "Keep adding, keep walking, keep advancing; do not stop, do not turn back, do not turn from the straight(direct) road."

Your desires are manifest one single breath at a time. This is the only way to guarantee the ultimate success of your desire. Simply ask yourself, "What can I do right now, for the next twenty minutes, to bring me closer to my goal?" Write it down!

CHAPTER XIV

Recognition

•

*The real voyage of discovery consists not in seeking
new landscapes but in having new eyes.*

—MARCEL PROUST

閒

Recently-while on a flight from Chicago to Jackson
Hole, Wyoming-Mike, the pilot asked me to join him in
the co-pilot's seat. The twin engine Cessna held eight
passengers with one extra seat up front.

As we began our descent into the mountain top pass,
he aligned the nose of the plane with the runway and
called my attention to a bank of lights that stood to the
base of the flight line.

At first glance, the distant lights appeared white in
color though only seconds later- thanks to gusting
winds-the signal lights had changed to green then to red
and back again to white. "That signal tells us if we are in
the correct position to land", Mike explained.

Initially, I wondered how the light could interpret our
position and relay back its findings? Was there some

kind of radar or radio sensor in the nose of the plane?

As the runway lay just in front of us, the light was green and the landing was perfect.

Walking to the hangar, I asked Mike about the changing lights. "What's up with those landing lights?"

"The V.A.S.I. (Vertical Approach Slope Indicator) is a fixed light. If we come in too high, we get a white reading, too low, and we would only see the red of the lights. When you're right on, you get the green light to land." He continued, "The lights are fixed and constant, it is the position of the plane that changes."

All along, it was my perception of the V.A.S.I. that was changing, not the lights themselves. As we adjusted our vertical approach-with the help of the blowing winds-the lights were our immediate feedback, continually allowing us to check our landing progress. By focusing on our immediate goal, the indicator kept us on course.

Once we *decided* on our goal, landing the airplane safely, we then *initiated* our game plan-reducing our airspeed and lowering our landing gear. The next step was to *recognize our feedback.*

Just as pilots constantly check the V.A.S.I. from their current point of view, so to do we need to check our actions and determine if they are moving us closer to our goal. Are the winds of change blowing us off course or are we where we need to be?

Thomas Carlyle suggests that "our main business is not to see what lies dimly at a distance, but to do what lies clearly at hand."

Having chosen to manifest the ultimate *desire* in your life-and in doing so liberating your self-you need to check the accumulation of your 20 Minute Victories and make certain that they are keeping us on course; *dies diem docet*—"the day teaches the day."

While recognizing the results of your current actions, you can always decide in the moment if you are heading in the right direction. If your present position is contrary to where you want to be, you simply adjust your movements to fit your overall plan.

Unless we change our direction, we are likely to end up where we are headed. So goes the ancient Chinese proverb, If Mike had chosen to ignore the original V.A.S.I. signal of the white light we would have flown over the runway. Had our position permitted us to view a red light and we opted not to adjust our course, we would have landed in the grassy field short of the flight line. By constantly checking our current position in relationship to our ultimate goal, we were able to hit the target we had been aiming at all along. *Recognizing our feedback* meant the difference between crashing and a safe landing.

At this point, the similarity between the V.A.S.I. and our own recognition of the feedback, ends. The feedback that we are alluding to is of the internal, NOT the external mode. We are addressing the feedback of the intuition not of outside opinion and conjecture. Remember, when it comes to *recognizing feedback,* no one gives you better direction than your self. Your V.A.S.I. is in your self. Your mandate comes from your gut. To follow external dictates is to miss the mark.

"We forfeit our uniqueness" wrote Vincent Van Gogh "by compromising and making concessions, today in this matter, tomorrow in another, according to the dictates (and feedback) of the world-by never contradicting the world, and by always following public opinion." The great artist deeply realized the danger of adherence to an external direction or mandate. He listened to and relied upon is own intuition (his own V.A.S.I.) to cast the only vote that mattered.

"Give me directions", they asked of Epictetus. "Why should I give you directions? Has not Zeus given you directions? Has he not given you what is your own free from hindrance and free from impediment? What directions then, what kind of orders did you bring when you came from him? Keep by every means what is your own; do not desire what belongs to others".

Both individuals *re-cognized* the importance of relying on that which they have possessed since birth. Feedback can only be judged in the light cast by one's own intuition. The feedback we are waiting for can only come from our own hearts. The rest is merely conjecture and simple opinion.

In his essay, *On Thinking for Yourself,* (Translated in Essays and Aphorisms by R.J. Hollingdale) Schopenhauer offers us this additional piece of evidence. "As the biggest library, if it is in disorder, is not as useful as a small but well arranged one, so you may accumulate a vast amount of knowledge but it will be of far less value to you than a much smaller amount if you have not thought it over for yourself; because only through ordering what you know by comparing every truth with every other truth can you take complete (direct) possession of your knowledge and get it into your power."

As is often the case, I find that Goethe leaves us a powerful hint: "To know your powers, look in your mind, not from me starts your creation. In my words you'd feel confined. Go to God for inspiration." He suggests that we "Go(return) to God for inspiration."

With this thought fresh in mind, let's take a moment to look at the words "inspiration" and "intuition."

To "in-spire" simply means to "re-in-fuse" the mind with your original dreams. The word "inspiration" comes form the Latin word *inspirare:* to breathe. It is closely linked with the word "enthusiasm": to "be inspired or possessed by the God within."

To free ourselves from the tyranny of the status quo we must first set our sights "in-wardly" by *re-cognizing* the signals that are supplied and dispensed enthusiastically by our own intuition.

Now the etymology of the word "intuition" also offers us an important clue. It comprises the words "in" and the word "tuition" or "to protect or to look after." True security and therefore protection-like the ultimate truth itself-comes from within You. By inhaling and supplying oxygen to the God within, your authentic self is resuscitated, empowered and sits anxiously awaiting the implementation of your natural resources.

The beginning of all life-biologically or spiritually-begins with a breath. "As the whisper in the cemetery offered, "The proof of this lies close at hand". Let's check the proof.

Close your eyes, inhale fully through your nose and draw your breath deep into your lungs. You will begin to feel your diaphragm, and therefore your stomach, slightly extend and protrude.

Hold that inhale for the count of four and then simply relax. Let the air in your lungs rush out through your nose like an inflated balloon that's been let go.

Notice how the outside world-with all of its expert opinions and well clarified theories, seems to fade away. As you begin to slowly repeat the above cycle of breath, listen to the faint whisper that remains. Ask yourself, "Based on my current feedback, am I moving closer to the achievement of my goal? Yes or no?" Is there something else I need to do in this current moment?"

By listening to and *re-cognizing* or re-membering your original-pre suffocation voice-you reawaken your "gut instinct" from its dormant slumber. Once tapped, your ultimate drive strengthens with each and every use. As it grows, soon no mask or facade can contain it.

Your intuition, and your mind for that matter, like the various muscles in your body, are subject to progressive adaptation and therefore grow stronger with each application. Each time they are called upon to perform, they gain strength and stamina.

By listening and subscribing to the voice at your center, the falcon begins to once again hear the call of the falconer. You may recall the foreboding lines of *Yeats's*

The Second Coming:

Turning and turning in the widening gyre
The falcon cannot hear the falconer;

The only true form of in-spiration and enthusiasm (in-thusiasm) is that which calls forth from your heart, that feeling that is born in your gut. What was your purpose before *Chatterdom* interfered? Clearly focused and committed to those beliefs that lie at your core, certain events begin to pull you in the direction of your destiny.

In ancient Sanskrit there is a term "Dharma", translated it means "duty." Your dharma, your duty, is your destiny, it is the contemplation of and the completion of your inner calling. Thankfully, we do not have to search very far. Your dharma is encoded and *re-cognized* as your heart's ultimate desire.

Now, your heart's desire, once awakened and emancipated, strives for the reunification with the universal Desire. As your inner voice calls out, your future begins to pull you towards your inevitable destiny. Like two magnets working on each other, when you begin to follow the direction of Your inner voice, you are pulled into the future, one breath at a time.

As if a skier being tugged by a ski boat, or its winter counterpart being drawn to the bottom of the mountain by the forces of gravity, deciding to liberate your ultimate desire, pulls you-like a river to the ocean-through the lefts and rights, ups and down's, the "this ways" and "that ways" of outside criticism and conjecture.

Your *in-tuition,* resuscitated by Your breath, offers

you the only true direction out of the "dark labyrinth" of survival. The world is full of outside knowledge and "expert opinion." Ignore the mob, the herd the gang. *Recognize* the feedback that lies in front of you, and then cast the only vote that really matters.

The tethers of outside influence are many. With each focused, deep breath you cut a chord that binds you, a chord that has heretofore held you prisoner. With each passing breath, your intuition is aroused and as such, *recognizes* the pull of your future destiny, of your heart's desire. There is no better partner. You'll see. Don't take my word for it. Investigate for yourself. Do it. Just breath.

CHAPTER XV

Evaluation

•

Do not look where you fall, but where you slipped.

—AFRICAN PROVERB

*In the days of adversity, do not forget
the days of prosperity.*

—ECCLESIASTICS

困

Evening was but a quarter of an hour away. The drive westbound on Canyon Rd. is a beautiful one. Facing into the Flatirons, one can't help noticing the snow capped peaks of the brilliant Continental Divide posing directly behind the foothills of Boulder, Colorado.

This particular late afternoon, both sides of the road were lined with hastily parked cars; their flashing hazards-scattered in a zig-zag pattern along Canyons' shoulders. The drivers, all standing alongside of their abandoned vehicles, gazing and pointing ahead.

Instantly, I began searching out the red emergency lights of the police car or ambulance. For sure, I would soon be able to see the bright, amber-orange glow of a road flare. No doubt, all of these impromptu spectators must be viewing an accident of some type. Was everyone okay, would the road be blocked for long?

To my surprise, there was no accident to investigate. There were no fire trucks or paramedics busily working on injured motorists. No patrol officer interviewing witnesses. There was however, a scene.

In my initial hurried state, I failed to recognize that which was the source of the audiences' awe and amazement. The sun had begun to set and the long shadows of the mountain ranges crept ever eastward. Nature-disregarding the fact that it had been overcast throughout the day-had prepared a brilliant spectacle for all who cared to watch. Once again I realized that for those of us who care to reduce our pace, the complexity and magnificence of nature always holds a lesson to be learned.

The scattered rays of sunlight broke through the clouds as if purposefully hand picking just certain portions of the mountains face to illuminate. The radiant colors of splendid yellow, orange, and light reddish-purple fashioned a delicate ladder stretching earthward from a partially obscured heaven; its entrance a smiling, thin crescent.

Smaller, billowing clouds set below the opaque blanket, appeared to act as a mirror, reflecting back the luminous beauty into the fountainhead of light. The sky was ablaze.

Legions of distant clouds timidly, challenged and encroached the fiery source. Ever so slowly, the sun dipped onto the western horizon, briefing revealing its face through a velvet fissure, gloating as if to say "I am the artist, behold my work and my signature."

Over time, I've witnessed many sunsets yet none will rival this particular night's beginning. It has since dawned on me just how fortunate we were to have had that evening heralded by a cloudy afternoon. Had it been perfectly clear, and minus the creative touch of the clouds, the sun would have left this day as a bright yellow ball, too powerful indeed, to have been viewed directly. The clouds, in disputing the authority of the sun's rays, guaranteed its brilliance.

Looking back over your life, have not some of your greatest accomplishments and achievements been secured on days with less than clear sailing, when your path was obscured in some inconvenient fashion? How many times have you come to the end of a challenging day, proud of the fashion in which you scaled and handled the mountains blocking your way? Do we not shine the greatest when we are challenged the most?

"Into every life a little rain must fall" is not a threat. Most certainly it is a promise. A promise made good by time.

Happiness and contentedness are not realized at the tedious and boring hands of an obstacle free life. The space before a hurdle is not meant to discourage us. It is more the spring board to satisfaction and learning. As the proverb goes, "Misfortune does not always come to injure", nor did the clouds that afternoon in Boulder come to ultimately ruin the sunset. Obstacles become impassable only for the impatient.

After having chosen your *direction, initiated your game plan* and having *recognized your feedback,* you can then begin to *evaluate your mistakes.*

In any worthwhile journey there will always be hurdles or stumbling blocks to traverse. Odysseus had the Cyclops, Theseus the Minotaur and Jason the Symplegades; each of these roadblocks were used as an incitement to propel the hero forward. How about some of the roadblocks in your life? How many times in the past have you successfully negotiated a barrier to your desire? Maybe it was a time constraint, a financial concern, a physical hurdle. In the end, were you not successful?

According to Thomas Carlyle, "The block of granite that was an obstacle in the pathway of the weak becomes a stepping stone in the pathway of the strong." Within every adversity there lies an equal or greater opportunity. We are but the pupils of our own mistakes.

How can one begin to learn from these "teachers", these obstacles or stumbling blocks? Epictetus answers this question in the following manner.

"It is circumstances that show us what we are. Therefore when a difficulty falls upon you, remember that God, like a trainer of wrestlers, has matched you with a rough (opponent). 'For what purpose?' you may say. Why, that you may become an Olympic conqueror; but it is not accomplished without sweat. In my opinion no one has had a more profitable difficulty than you have had, if you choose to make use of it as an athlete would deal with a young antagonist."

Centuries later, the Abolitionist Frederick Douglas knew that if there were "no struggle", there certainly would be "no progress."

Isn't it true that your struggles, your daily trials and tribulations possess a certain tutorial quality? James Joyce believed that a "genius makes no mistakes. His(her) errors are volitional and are the portals of discovery".

Even so, we label (or libel) our obstacles and mistakes as calamities and failures; thus discarding them before any valuable hint or lesson can be obtained. In the quest to *evaluate your mistakes*, it is your perception that will be altered, not the events themselves. As Milton coaches us in Book one of *Paradise Lost:*

A mind not to be chang'd by Place or Time.
The mind is its own place, and in it self
Can make a Heav'n of Hell, a Hell of Heav'n.

In *evaluating our mistakes,* if we view them as failures, we remand ourselves to hell. If our mind can find no benefit from the lesson of a particular error or miscue, than we will not see the heaven of learning.

Fortunately, it is your mind that dictates your attendance in either the comfortable bliss of paradise(learning) or the doubting turmoil's of hell(failure).

If our residence in hell is the fault of our thoughts and mis-directed beliefs, how is it then that we may free ourselves from this mental Hades. My grandfather often told me that "haste makes waste", and that if I found myself in the middle of an error or a mistake, it was more than likely do to a "rash action or decision". He would admonish me to "slow down and pay attention to what lies at hand."

Often times, our speed prohibits us from recognizing the clues and hints that lead to success. Hastily, we view a mistake as a worthless error and therefore remand ourselves to the hell of failure.

The ancient sage Heraclitus leaves us this clue. "Most people do not take heed of the things they encounter, nor do they grasp them even when they have learned about them, although they suppose they do."

Alternately, we are elevated to heaven when-void of blinding speed and haste-we review the circumstances of our current situation in the light of specific reason. By slowing down, paying attention to, and specifically evaluating our mistakes, we will always be able to identify the inherent suggestions and lessons of our initial errors.

Slow down for a moment, close your eyes, breath deeply and focus on your mistake. With the situation front and center in your mind's eye ask yourself the following questions.

"What-specifically-can I learn from the mistake at hand?"

"What exact lessons are my current circumstances attempting to teach me?"

"Is it not possible to use this exercise to shed some light on a more advantageous course?"

Now with the answers fresh in mind, is it at all possible to add one or all of them to your list of 20 Minute

Victories. What did you learn? What new action has become clearer in light of this current mis-take? Do you have a new 20 Minute Victory?

Must we judge our mistakes and errors at face value. Couldn't we hold them beneath the microscope of reason and discover the valuable lessons they possess? Regardless of the errors we make, "we master fortune by accepting" them and viewing them as tutors.

As is often the case, I think back to that night in the cemetery and recall the thoughts of the guiding voice; "All errors are initial."

That afternoon in Boulder, ultimately the sun presented itself, proving it had been victorious in arresting the multitudes of obstructing clouds.

Throughout life, our signature will reflect our receptive, embracing attitude toward our own clouds, and not the fabrications we contrive in an attempt to avoid them.

Notice that when you challenge your self-perceived obscurities, initial errors and informative mistakes, they too will drift away like a wind borne cloud. Only then will your inherent potential shine through.

Chapter XVI

Consideration

•

*When one door of happiness closes, another opens, but
often we look so long at the closed door that we do not
see the one that has been opened for us.*

—Hellen Keller

閏

Cardinals sing a morning song as loud and rousing as
that of the most trumpeting rooster. Every day-just about
6:30 am-the fire engine red bird began his chorus just
outside my window. Perched on a nearby branch, his
perfect timing and blazing volume so dependable, seldom was I in need of an alarm clock.

After the first couple of mornings, I noticed that the
grosbeak's verse and rhyme were punctuated by a loud,
dull "thump". After two or three choruses of chirping,
there was a secondary pause followed by a blunt "thud".
A conductor's baton could not have orchestrated a
smoother flow.

"Whistle, whistle, whistle, whistle...thump", then a
"Whistle, whistle, whistle, whistle...thud". This would
go on, every morning, for three quarters of an hour or

more.

At the end of the fourth week, curiosity got the best of me and I decided to catch the cardinal in the act. At revelry, I jumped out of bed, and exited the side door of my house so as not to confront the finch directly. True to form his song began. "Whistle, whistle, whistle ..."

ahah! The "thump" had finally been identified.

It seems that the persistent little cardinal saw its own reflection in the closed window. Its song was more like a war cry, and at its completion, the Kamikaze bird would fly directly at the intruder in the window. Head-or maybe beak-first, the tiny combatant consistently charged straightway at its opponent. Never realizing that he was his own worst enemy (and I'm sure there is a lesson for us to learn in that), the valiant bird circled momentarily before commencing its repeated dive at its own reflection.

After endless attacks, the pointed plumage of the aggressors head lay matted and flat. Worried for the birds safety, I ran inside to open the window in hopes of removing its mirrored foe. As I cranked the window open the deep belly chirping ceased.

Believing that he had successfully routed the trespasser from its perch, he went on about his business, only to return the following morning to resume its never ending battle. Throughout that summer on North Captiva Island, the tiny warrior never missed a morning.

I often wonder about the consistency of that little bird. Time and time again he would confront and then attack the reflected cardinal. His success realized only by outside intervention.

I recalled the times in my life where blind, persistent repetition of a useless or outdated thought or action, served only to increase my stamina, though seldom my station. Repeating (or reliving) old, questionable beliefs and habits seemed easier than creating new ones, regardless of their potential success.

The bird did not know any better and neither had I; many a day I spent bouncing my head against the wall. Suffering from the blind viewpoint of mindless consistency, I believed that keeping my nose to the stone would bring success; never realizing that such tunnel vision indeed kept me busy, though I seemed destined to "work harder not smarter."

"There are those who would mis-teach us, that to stick in a rut is consistency-and a virtue, and that to climb out of a rut is inconsistency-and a vice". Mark Twain was not the only one to recognize the importance of fresh thought and the power of new ideas. Emerson-thirty years Twain's senior-warned us that consistency, a "foolish (bird-brained) consistency is the hobgoblin of little minds...With consistency a great soul has simply nothing to do...Speak what you think now in hard words and tomorrow speak what to-morrow thinks in hard words again, though it contradict everything you said to-day."

More recently, Aldous Huxley worried that repetition and consistency are "contrary to nature"

Today, examples abound in the definition of an unnatural, "foolish consistency". It seems our goal is to remain counter to our own natural potential to think unique thoughts. In an attempt to be consistent with our neighbor, we dress in someone else's fashion, subscribe to antiquated thoughts and are ruled by the obsolete and archaic canons of the mob, the herd, the gang, the clique, the cult; all in an attempt to conform and "fit in."

We labor in the rut of the "tried and true", we live our lives "better safe than sorry" and all around us lay the ruins of a philosophical "one in the hand is worth two in the bush". The mob as gained another convert. To busy, time and time again, doing what were told, we seldom get the chance to think a fresh thought, to try a new way, to venture into the unknown.

Authenticity and uniqueness are voted upon-and vetoed-by the collective. The only description of a thought is the copied prescription of our visionless neighbor. We grow content repeatedly duplicating and plagiarizing the actions of another, simply because we are comfortable with them.

The sightless repetition-again and again-of that which we are accustomed to is not courageous; not at all; the habitude of blind compliance serves only to dis-courage our ultimate success. Day in and day out we willingly subjugate ourselves to the ever popular, time tested theories. The duplication-ad ditto-of these exercises never moves us closer toward our authentic goal. Our routines and habits serve only to anesthetize our souls.

Having chosen your ultimate *desire* and then *initiated* your plan of action-all the while *recognizing* your feedback and subsequently *evaluating* your mistakes-there comes a point when you can look to change or alter your actions. There comes a time to *consider additional options.*

Suppose you decided to travel to Florida and the morning of your departure your car broke down, could you not consider additional modes of transportation to get you to gator country? Maybe you could fly, take a train or even a boat?

My point is simple. There may come a time when you will need to consider an additional avenue to propel you toward your goal.

Considering additional options has nothing to do with the abandonment of your goal. You are simply giving yourself permission, and exercising your right, to choose an alternate course. Though, to some this may appear a vice or as the surrendering of our goals, nothing is farther from reality.

Even in ancient times the Roman playwright Terrence knew that "nobody ever drew up their plans for life so well but what the facts, and the years, and experience always introduce some modification."

Robert Louis Stevenson expands on this position. "To hold the same view(point) at forty as we held at twenty is to have been stupefied for a score of years and to take rank, not as a prophet, but as an unteachable brat, well birched and none the wiser".

Be it twenty years or twenty minutes, if you choose- after having *recognized your feedback* and *evaluated your mistakes*—to *consider additional options,* or to create a varied viewpoint, this is most certainly a virtue, not a vice.

What good is it to consistently travel aboard a train

that you find to be on the wrong track? or to run down a path that leads you astray form your destiny?

Narrow-mindedness might build stamina, but if it ultimately leads us away form our goal or contrary to your dharma, of what specific benefit is it to us? Only the fool(or the cardinal) ignores the opportunity for modification.

To be mis-directed is to refuse the benefits that accompany a flexible point of view. Goethe warns us that "we must always change, renew, rejuvenate ourselves; otherwise we harden."

Just as a gymnast must stretch his/her body in order to be able to compete, so too can you and I stretch our thoughts and viewpoints and remain contrary to the stiff and rigid convictions of yesterday.

The Koran suggests that God will not change our condition until we change what is in ourselves. Plato tells us that "All things that have a soul change, and possess in themselves a principle of change, and in changing move according to the law and to the order of destiny".

Let's not gloss over this thought. According to the great philosopher, there can be no fulfillment of ones destiny in the absence of adjustment and modification. There can be no true dharma in the absence of deference.

By *considering additional options,* you participate in the natural flow of events. Hampered by the stagnant complacency of consistency, there is no forward progress. To create is "to cause growth", and to stagnate is to stifle that progress. Without change there can be no growth.

"Today is not yesterday. We ourselves change."
Thomas Carlyle new of the importance of *considering
additional options* and questions us further. "How then,
can our works and thoughts continue always the same?
There can be no acting or doing of any kind, till it be re-
cognized that there is a thing to be done; the thing once
re-cognized, doing in a thousand shapes becomes possible."

If the caterpillar were content with its status quo, we
would be robbed of the beauty of her intricately colorful
wings. So to do we preclude ourselves from the master-
piece of a brilliant life by constantly remaining bird
brained and deeply bogged in adherence. Void of the lat-
itude to adopt a different course, we slowly begin to
manacle and imprison ourselves.

Compliance is thought to be safer-and most certainly
easier-than creation. Worried that others might view us
as whimsical, "wishy-washy" or erratic, we loose the
forest in order to stand with the trees.

Troubled by the persuasions of *Chatterdom*—be it the
continual internal dialogue of our own negativity or the
bombardment of the external ramblings of the "experts"
in our lives-we remain stuck in the bog of consistency,
even though it calls us away from our own hearts. Once
again, we trade living for surviving.

How is it then, that one might aspire to a life that does
not fear flexibility and change? In order to experience
your courage, you must act courageously. "Don't be too
timid and squeamish about your actions" Emerson tells
us. "All life is an experiment. The more experiments you
make the better".

Throughout the D.I.R.E.C.T. Acronym, there is no greater "workout" or "experiment" than *considering additional options.*

Ask yourself, "Based on the current feedback, coupled with the lessons of my mis-takes, what different approach can I take to move me closer to my goal"?

Pose this question to yourself, "What if I were to .....? and then fill in the dots.

Check those things that Providence has supplied you and then ponder a different viewpoint form where to embark.

"Currently, I am here. But what would happen if I were to....? Think about it. Consider additional options.

You are not being called upon to change the ultimate goal. You are simply being challenged to investigate an alternative course based on the hints and suggestions that your intuition has supplied in the aftermath of *recognizing feedback* and *evaluating mistakes.*

When was the last time you were confronted with a combination lock or a padlock and a fist full of keys? As you spun the various numbers-first left than right-or attempted different keys-try the long silver one or the shiny gold Quickset-isn't it true that your desire to remove the lock remained constant? Did you abandon your attempt to gain entry or did you keep considering additional combinations or keys?

The emancipation of your ultimate desire is no different. The pull of your destiny remains constant, while you simply consider additional avenues or paths that place you in greater relationship with that pull. Say to yourself,

"This particular set of lefts and rights, ups and downs have not provided me with the advancement I had initially hoped for. What additional options do I currently possess?"

Raise your sail one foot and you get ten feet of wind, so is the Chinese proverb. Experimentation is the key. By *considering additional options,* you begin to experiment and trade that which has not worked here-to-fore, for that which might in the future. We gain experience through this trial and error. With the lessons of chance, another teacher awaits you.

William James suggests that a definition of "Genius" is one who perceives a situation in a "un-habitual way". What are some of the additional options that you are currently considering? Is there a way to view your current journey in an "un-habitual way?" How is it possible to apply your natural resources in a courageously new and ingenious way?

We learned earlier that once our mind is stretched and flexed it never regains its "original dimensions". Consider this question:

"What new approach can I employ-right now-for the next 20 minutes, to move me closer to my destiny?" If only the persistent cardinal could have considered such a question. Flexibility and adaptation are the cornerstones of *inlightenment.*

Chapter XVII

Tenacity

•

*The heights by great men(women) reached and kept
were not attained by sudden flight. But they, while their
companions slept, were toiling upward in the night.*

—Longfellow

*The strength of our virtue should not be measured by
our special exertions, but by our habitual acts.*

—Pascal

困

The early morning hours of a recent spring day once
again reminded me of the various lessons nature has to
offer if one will simply slow down long enough to be a
student. We need only search the crocheted doily to learn
the thoughts of the spider, or behold a hand-crafted bas-
ket in hopes of enjoying the sparrow.

How would I forget nature's cardinal, the sunset or the
night in the cemetery?

My teacher this day would be a small yet mighty creature, a bee-more specifically a yellow jacket. Many of us

know personally just how tenaciously ferocious this meek little insect can become when it is forced to defend itself.

Thanks to a mishap at the tender young age of six, I learned not to stick crabapples into wholes in the ground. Since learning this lesson at the hands-or better yet-at the stinging tails of some 150 teachers that late summer afternoon, my phobia has grown into a powerful one. The drone and thrum of their flapping wings immediately transport me back in time.

I lay paralyzed, the covers pulled up just below my nose. The sounds of the buzzing menace were more reminiscent of the thunder of an airplane's engines.

Circling the room in an attempt to free himself, the flying terror descended-in a dive bombing fashion-towards the opened screen window just above my half hidden head.

Apparently, the bees know-as you and I-the brilliance, power and seemingly medicinal qualities of our Sun. The obscurity produced with the absence of the sun is feared by all the inhabitants of our planet.

In a dauntless attempt to return to the Source, the yellow jacket fought valiantly to regain its direct relationship with its life giving energy. Frantically searching the screen for any opening that would lead to the radiant sun and to his freedom, this dance went on for over twenty minutes.

For what seemed an eternity, I was incapacitated with fear, Eventually, I summoned enough courage and developed a game plan. As the yellow jacket made his pass and crossed the bookcase at the foot of the bed, I was almost ready to make my move.

This time, as he hit the screen, I threw off the covers, leaped to my knees and slammed the sliding window closed. The flying menace was trapped between the screen and the newly shut plate glass window. Victory and safety were finally at hand. I had confronted the enemy and he was mine.

Later that same morning I returned to the scene expecting to find the yellow wasp still imprisoned; personally having dealt with the karmic ramifications for my earlier actions. Surprisingly enough, he was gone. I checked the sliding window track, each of the four corners and every inch of the screen. In the upper left hand corner there was a small whole in the webbing; apparently large enough for the bee to escape. My prisoner had gained-quite possibly tunneled-his way to freedom.

The words of George Bernard Shaw whispered to mind. "The people who get on in this world are the people who get up and look for the circumstances they want, and if they can't find them, they make them."

Sliding the window shut, I compelled the incarcerated insect to either find an escape or create one. With his retreat being cut off by the window, he had no choice but to tenaciously move forward, no alternative other than to advance.

The learned habit of buzzing the room in search of the answers to his dilemma no longer possible. His solution lay within the power of the present and the mystery of his immediate future.

Does the bee's struggle for freedom and his quest in the direction of the sun seem at all like your own journey towards inlightenment? How long have you been buzzing around looking for a way to free yourself from life's turmoil all the while hoping to gain entrance into the light?

How many times have you retreated into the habits of the past, blindly following the voluminous ideas of the mob, failing to realize that the answers you seek are directly in front of you?

When the bee was cut off from retreat, and forced to focus in the limited space of the present, only then did he obtain his freedom. With a flexible stoutness, the tenacious creature directly combed each and every individual tiny square of the screen until he had achieved his release into the light. There was no surrender, only tenacity.

The final letter in the Direct acronym stands for *Tenacity*. Having identified your *true desire, initiated your game plan, evaluated your mistakes, recognized your feedback* and *subsequently considered additional options,* there comes a time for simple *tenacity*.

The Sufi proverb tells us that the constant dripping of water wears away the mighty stone. Like the rain attacking the pyramid of earth that night in the cemetery, the tenacious exercise and application of your 20 Minute Victories, will begin to erode the "marble" that blocks the manifestation of your *dharma*. The steady and regular employment of your natural resources leads you over

B.P. BRAWDY

closer to achieving your goal.

Once again, the physical exercise phenomenon known as Progressive Adaptation also is applicable here. Each and every time you utilize your Natural Resources in conjunction with your 20 Minute Victories, your innate capacity multiplies and strengthens. You grow increasingly familiar with your true potential each and every time you call upon it.

Now the difference between the powers of tenacity and the mind numbing repetition of the "tried and true" can best be described by the Spanish philosopher George Santayana in his *The life of Reason: Reason in Common Sense.* "Fanaticism consists in redoubling your effort when you have forgotten your aim.." Sound familiar? It reminds me of the old traveler's saying, 'We're lost, but we're making record time.'

Suppose one were to sit in front of a piano and continually strike the same key. Soon you will have perfected the motion needed to produce a musical note, though if that one note is not produced in concert with other notes, you will have no song. "Da, da, da, da, da" ad infinitum.

Callused as your one finger may be from the repetitive striking of a lone key, failing to continually re-consider or re-evaluate this single tone in relationship to the ultimate aim of producing music, one develops a mental carpal tunnel syndrome. Soon the mind becomes rigid and incapable of further experimentation or movement.

Tenacity-unlike the visionless *re-petition* of habit and conformity-relies upon the constant *re-cognition* of feedback as viewed in the light of your intuition. Your success is not based upon the blind reproduction of action or repetitive motions and thoughts, rather your progress is charted by the faithful *re-examination* of your current location or station in relationship to your ultimate goal.

By replicating or folding your experimental actions back onto your original goal, it acts as a template. This constant comparison allows you to continually *re-evaluate* or *re-consider* your current position relative to our ultimate destiny.

Being tenaciously creative in the current moment, guards against the deterioration and atrophy of your dreams. Ask yourself, "Am I moving closer to or farther away from my intended end by the employment of this current action?" Based on your answer, pose yourself this question.

"With what I have just learned, how can I create a new 20 Minute Victory?" Once you have your answer, add it to your list.

The 18th Century French philosopher Voltaire writes, "Perfection is attained by slow degrees; it requires the hand of time."

Contrary to how it may appear at first glance, there are no "overnight successes." Counter to the popular belief in *Chatterdom,* there is no "instant stardom." *Flying colors are crawling colors.*

"Nothing great," Epictetus offers, "is produced suddenly, since not even the grape or the fig is. If you say to me now that you want a fig, I will answer to you that it requires time: let it flower first, then put forth fruit, then ripen".

Baltasar Gracian in the *Art of Worldly Wisdom* suggests "...wait, for it marks a great heart endowed with patience; never to be in undue haste, or excited....A prudent waiting brings season to accomplishment and ripeness to what is hidden. The crutch of time accomplishes more than the iron club of Hercules. Fortune herself crowns patience with the heaviest of garlands".

This is an important distinction. Tenacity does not mean impatience. By continually testing your 20 Minute Victory, vis-à-vis, your ultimate desire coupled with the current lesson of Nature, your focus is one of applied persistence not blind repetition.

If genius is achieved by the contemplation of situations in "un-habitual ways", than heroism (heroinism) is attained by the tenacious application of those unique thoughts.

"The characteristic of heroism is its persistency. When you have chosen your part abide by it, and do not weakly attempt to reconcile yourself with the world." Ralph Waldo Emerson continues, "...that which we persist in doing becomes easier-not that the Nature of the task has changed, but our ability to do it has increased". Once again we are confronted with the understanding of progressive adaptation.

Your 20 Minute Victories-through the psychological process of stress and adaptation-elevates you to the role of hero or heroine. Goethe believed, "Austere perseverance.. (direct) and continuous effort, may be employed by the least of us and rarely fails of its purpose, for its silent power grows irreversibly greater with time".

If "time heals all wounds" then time also "guarantees all goals" to those who persevere. In the quest of any goal, the true test of courage is tenacity. Through insightful perseverance, success is always at hand.

We know that *inlightenment* takes place in the present and that *Inlightenment* is to that instant, what the Years are to the minute. With the tenacious application of your dharma's game plan, come the helping hands of Mother Nature and Father Time.

PART
4

THE EPILOGUE

Chapter XVIII

The End of the Tunnel

•

In anything at all perfection is finally attained not when there is no longer anything to add, but when there is no longer anything to take away, when a body has been stripped down to its nakedness.

—Saint Exuprey

困

 For many of us, the above quote-taken from *Wind, Sand and Stars*—can, at first reading at least, seem contrary to all that we have been taught. Perfection, excellence, wholeness and lofty merit have always been a distant goal whose attainment was based on the accumulation of various traits and successes.

The American architect and engineer R. Buckminster Fuller believed that we are all "born geniuses" and that "Society de-geniuses" us. Imagine that. Each of us is born with an extraordinary intellectual power and that over the course of learning we forget those capabilities. From birth, you have possessed all the natural resources and raw materials (genius) you need to live a perfect life. So what happened?

Has your education stifled you, and in doing so, have you been "de-geniused"? Have the truths that you adopted in the name of learning, served to imprison you in a suffocating ignorance? Has the mob been your only teacher?

YOU were born an Artist, do you remain so today? YOU were a genius at birth, are you really any different now?

Like the surface of a tabletop continually subject to repainting, is your "natural grain" and beauty hidden by the accumulated plaque and debris of scholastic instruction? Was Thoreau correct when he offered that "it is only when we forget all of our learning that we truly begin to know"?

Suppose all the years of education have left you wandering in the dismal labyrinth of your own wasteland? Have you learned how not to be a genius? Have you forgotten just how to be an artist. Have you learned apathy, resignation and conformity in place of creativity, spontaneity and individualism?

Instead of cultivating the inborn knowledge that we possess, we seek to concoct, fabricate or manufacture it. We covet the Guru's clothing, mimic his/her mannerisms and gymnastics and adopt their culinary peculiarities.

All this "learning" adds weight to the mask. Painfully, we fail to re-cognize that the path to truth lies close at hand. As Dante offers us, "Everything, by an impulse of its own nature(not at the prodding of an "expert"), tends toward perfection....Everything is at its best and most perfect when it is in the condition intended for it by the First Cause."

It is hard to forget the admonition in the cemetery; "Opaqueness gains strength in distance." The more distance placed between yourself and your "first cause", the more opaque your soul becomes. YOU were born an artist, do you remain so today?

How can we begin to forget those lessons that no longer serve us while searching for our Something To Believe In? How can we uneducate ourselves in the ways of the tribe? How can we reverse the negative effects of *Chatterdom*? Be it internal or external dialogue, how can we begin to free ourselves from its grasp? We begin with a closer look at the word education.

The word education, comes from the Latin *"educere"* or to "draw or lead forth, to bring out or develop from a latent condition." Therefore, to educate is to teach yourself and uncover the genius that lies within; that which is your "First Cause". All the knowledge and expertise you need resides within, *in-potentia* as a natural resource.

You might find this interesting also. The word for "truth" in ancient Greek—*Aletheia*—is translated as "The unconcealed." Now if our truth lies within us as potential unconcealed by the mask, than it is the excavation of that truth which is the only true education. To "draw or lead forth" the "unconcealed" from beneath the mask, this is the only way to reverse the lessons of *Chatterdom,* this is the sole way to re-discover your

Something To Believe In.

By peeling away the opaqueness of the guess work of the "herd", you begin to gain an insight into that that is true for you. Moreover, if your lesson was taught to you, it ultimately has no power for you. Only the lessons you have learned-and will learn in the future-can bring you strength.

Truth is not learned from the chalkboard or discerned from the printed page, only when one experiences knowledge and truth directly, does one understand. Second hand knowledge is but a fancy term for ignorance, for without direct knowledge there is only illusion. This understanding is also the basis of our legal system.

In any trial, the ultimate goal of a jury-or of the presiding judge-is to ascertain the truth based on the admissible evidence. Witnesses are called and under Direct examination they testify as to any *first hand* knowledge they may have in regard to the pending case.

Hearsay evidence-that evidence that is indirect ("Person A told me that person B said or did this, though I have no direct knowledge of person B's words or actions") is inadmissible and will not be considered by the judge or the jury.

These particular rules of evidence are also applicable in your own personal search for *Something To Believe In*. As you set out to locate the Truth, only that evidence obtained by direct examination-minus the vast speculations of the experts with their hearsay evidence-can be contemplated. The great mystic Meister Eckhart leaves us this clue "Whatever I want to express in it's truest meaning must emerge from within me and pass through an inner form. It cannot come from outside but must emerge from within."

The indirect beliefs and views of the sense driven intellectual inhabitants of *Chatterdom* mean little if not corroborated by your own instincts and intuition. Only direct knowledge yields the truth.

Imagine going to the beach for a walk and never removing your shoes. Would you have truly experienced the shore in all its delight without directly feeling the sand at your feet? By subscribing to the allusions of anothers' truth, we gain only an illusion for ourselves. When a perception is indirect it is a mistake.

In hopes of uncovering your Something To Believe In, you can search within for the ways of your heart; from *"cackling herd"* you gain conjecture, from yourself you experience the truth.

Jehovah's order to Abraham recorded in Genesis 12:1 is also helpful. "Get thee out of thy country, and from thy kindred, and from thy father's house..." Here is our direction to forget the teachings of our country, kindred and father. The way to "in-lightenment"(or "re-cognizing the light within") highlighted in his words. As Shakespeare writes, "Go to your bosom; Knock there, and ask your heart what it doeth know."

The only knowledge and understanding of the Truth is-forgive the play on words-'under' where you are 'standing' right now. Your goal is the eradication of those lessons and beliefs that imprison your inherent genius and squelch your true potential.

Knowledge is under your skull as well as under your skin. You need not search outside of yourself for truth and knowledge. They are born in your natural breath. If *in-telligence* is close at hand or right in front of our noses, than it is the breath (the inhalation of that which lies directly before you) that resuscitates your original genius. Once again the dance of life presents itself.

When Michelangelo wrote "with chisel in hand all is well", was he leaving us a clue? Was he suggesting that mental health and perfection can be maintained as long as we chisel away at the suffocating, marble-like lessons of the status quo? Can we employ the chisel to repel the "de-genius-ing" effects placed on us by society? Was this our admonition to unlearn that which we have learned? Truthfully, only you can tell.

The Crossroads

Your search for *Something To Believe In,* now compels you to make yet another decision. Having moved towards the proverbial "light at the end of the tunnel," you have emerged standing on a path that offers two alternate ways. You know firsthand the meaning of Robert Frost's poem *The Road Not Taken:*

Two roads diverged in a wood,
and I-
I took the one

Now you also stand at a fork in the road, a pivotal branching. To the right lies the indirect course of the formulated, "fictitious character."

On the left stretches the road seldom taken: the direct path of the natural or fundamental. The Indirect vs. the Direct. Inculcation vs. Re-Cognition. The Formulated vs. the Fundamental. Surviving as opposed to living. To fearfully be controlled by another or to courageously chart an authentic path. Herein resides your decision.

"God offers to every mind its choice between truth and repose. Take which you please; you can never have both." As Emerson suggests, eventually you will decide whether to (a) actively and directly uncover the truth-and in doing so liberate yourself from the ignorance you have adopted-or (b) remain in a state of laziness and fear thus guaranteeing a life-long imprisonment for your soul.

In terms of creative thought it seems so much easier to "go with the flow" and to refuse to "rock the boat"; ever loitering among the "shoulds" and "should nots", the "ought to's" and "ought not to's", the "musts" and "must nots" of the current cliques or cult.

Once again, Nature holds a clue. Like a virgin rain-drop turned into hail in the cumulonimbus clouds of a thunderstorm, we are battered about by the fluctuating and turbulent currents of outside conjecture and belief. Our continual collision with the alternating blows and ruffles of the "gurus" leaves us ever encased in a frozen "fictitious character," too stiff and inflexible to breathe a fresh thought.

In hopes of "fitting in," we construct-with the help of society-an "antithetical mask." We then employ this false self in an attempt to gain the approval of those whom we have chosen to follow; artistry replaced by acquiescence; liberty supplanted with a membership in the herd.

Conformity is chosen in place of creativity as the safer of the two options. Here our direct instincts and fundamental intuition are ignored in favor of popular opinion and the commands of prevailing cult. We follow the dots, stay between the lines; too timid to color outside of the circles.

The desperate struggle between these polarities leaves one tired and spent. For many of us it takes years before we realize just how futile our struggle has been.

Soon though, Nature begins to reassert herself and, like the Minotaur of Greek mythology-half human, half bull-eventually we awaken and find ourselves trapped in the bewildering labyrinth of life.

We find ourselves lost and confused by outside opinion, not knowing which way to turn. Half fundamental, half formulated, the apathetic part of us wants to be controlled or yoked like an animal in the field. All the while our fundamental self calls out to be free and void of our inauthentic and contrived lives. The struggle to survive versus the experience of life.

If Thoreau was correct and most of us indeed "lead lives of quiet desperation," it is because we find ourselves engulfed in the battle between the formulated mask and our fundamental voice.

In the search for knowledge and truth, will you rely on yourself-the "beat of your bosom"-or will you opt for the well-traveled route of lecture and conformity? The courageous life or the slothful blur? The decision is yours alone. Only through internal dialogue, will you begin to re-cognize the Epiphany.

Might you truly decide to command yourself directly thus forgetting the dictates and obstacles of the chattering mob-all possibilities become probabilities.

To finish the Robert Frost poem:

Two roads diverged in a wood,
and I-
I took the one less traveled by,
And that has made all the difference.

Obviously, my father decided to end his life the day he jumped. His struggle between the polarities became too much. For many of us, by rejecting the call of our heart, or by refusing to follow our "inward sun", we too commit suicide, though minus the dramatic flare of a biological death. Though a philosophical or emotional suicide, it is just as deadly nonetheless.

The incoming tide-with its devastating persistence and continuity-directly begins to dismantle the meticulous architecture of the sand castle, when the child's' plastic bucket is removed. Human emancipation from the womb is no different.

The final lunge of birth, is in fact, the first step towards death. The moon passes sentence and time is the executioner.

Each day we ignore our authentic dharma and opt for the lazy existence of inauthentic conformity, we too commit suicide. If "life is what we make of it" then death is simply life minus a direct plan.

Rollo May is even more direct. In his *"Man's Search for Meaning"* he makes clear that we as human beings cannot survive "in a condition of emptiness for very long." He goes on to say that "if we are not growing toward something", if we remain trapped in the facade, "we do not merely stagnate; the pent-up potentialities turn into morbidity and despair, and eventually into destructive activities."

If the afternoon reflects a morning spent in the directionless apathy of the status quo, pay close attention; for the smell of a philosophical death is soon discernible. It is fear, is the greatest immobilizer in life and the most powerful manacle of the human heart. Only the timid let life slip away. Only the weak follow the lethargic path of conformity and sloth. Only the fearful hide, when their whisper from within beckons them onward, contrary to the plea of *Chatterdom.*

Your search for *Something to Believe In* is actually a simple one. Its simplicity however can also become its down fall. In a time when high tech solutions and gadgets are believed to be the answer, the simplest of cures are very often overlooked. In hopes of discovering the "latest cure" or the "new and improved" answer to our current dilemmas, we search outside of ourselves for those things that reside within. If there is a magic bullet" or a "sure thing" in life, it will only be found in your heart.

So why have so many of us gone astray? How have so many of us forgotten who it is we truly are? Why are we forever removed from our Something to believe in?

I don't know. Maybe I never will. The question of its origin I will leave for greater minds than mine.

That being the case, I content myself these days with a more proactive approach to the void within. I content myself with the practice of Mind-Ups sm,.

MIND-Ups ^{SM}

As I have stated directly throughout this book, I am a strong proponent of your natural ability to create the life you desire. A life free from the negative effects of fear, stress, illness and apathy. I believe that there is no greater or more powerful force known to humankind today, than an individual suffused with his or her *Something To Believe In*.

The Chinese symbol decorating each chapter's title page, is one that spoke to me directly the day I first encountered it. It reminded me of a passage in Genesis (Gen. 2:9) "At the center of the garden he (God) placed the tree of life...."

Depending on whom you ask, this symbol stands for liberation, for surmounting challenges, for prevailing in the face of adversity, for overcoming life's obstacles, for the emancipation from one's self imposed prison. God "placed the tree" in the center. You and I have built the cage about it.

The four sides of the symbol represent the box, the facade, the cage, the container that many of us find ourselves today. At the center of the (garden) symbol stands the lonely sapling, the tiny tree imprisoned in the labyrinth of *Chatterdom*. It isn't dead, its in there, anxiously awaiting to be freed from its pen. Not unlike my grandmother's rose bushes, the tiny tree stands willing to greet the light of spring.

Mind-Ups^{SM} are the exercises we use in our Power of Purpose Workshops, to "free the tree". Plain and simple. Why Mind-Ups^{SM}? Because the mind is also a muscle. The mind, like any other muscle in your body, grows and adapts as long as it is challenged and nourished properly.

Many today are familiar with the concept of "working out" and with weight lifting routines and aerobic programs to build the body, yet few have chosen to extend their workout to include the mind. Sadly, very few of us "pump iron" for the brain.

Mind-Ups^{SM} are the brain's equivalents to the push-ups, sit-ups and pull-ups for the human body. Just as a well rounded physical fitness or postural alignment program sets out to build strength, flexibility and endurance-all the while reducing any extra fat stores-Mind-Ups(are exercises that are designed to increase the psychological and philosophical muscles of the human brain.

In addition to rebuilding these "mental muscles" to their

original power and suppleness, the drills also help to burn any deposits of "psycho fat or flab" that may be leaving you apathetic and listless.

As in any physical exercise routine, the need to develop a strong base is paramount. The Mind-Ups^{SM} agenda is no different. The drills-listed above-are used in a gradually adaptive format.

Because the mind is also a muscle, the guidelines of progressive adaptation work just as proficiently for the mind as they do for the musculature. With the concept of 20 Minute Victories, you can develop a personal routine with this steady, evenly paced progression in mind. Because the mind is also a muscle, "Use it or Lose it." As is atrophy in the body, so is atrophy in the mind. To be (fit) or not to be (fit) is solely up to you.

The following exercises are but a brief list of drills that will-if followed on a daily basis-begin to reverse the negative affects of stress and fear. Subsequently, they will afford you the strength, flexibility, and stamina to manifest your ultimate desire.

As you have no doubt sumized, the D.I.R.E.C.T. Acronym is one of the more comprehensive mental exercises in the Mind-Ups^{SM} program. It is designed to tap all of your natural resources and challenge you to employ your ultimate potential.

There are six basic more basic sets of Mind-Ups^{SM} exercises. Mental Imagery (Visualization), Inspiration (Breathing), Nourishment, Deeds, Utilities and Phase Outs.

The Mental Imagery exercises or visualizations deal
with the pictures you make in your mind. By "seeing"
yourself as if you have the intended desire already
achieved, it causes the mind to make additional connections between the billions of brain cells called neurons.
These additional couplings of cells and their pathways
build strength and flexibility. *Seeing is not only believing, seeing is becoming.* On most occasions, when I am
asked to define the mental imagery portion of the program, many are curious and want to "learn how to visualize." I offer to you-as I offer to them-the following.
You already know how to visualize. You are already an
expert at mental imagery. Oh no? Think back to the last
time you were affraid, angry, depressed, offended. You
see, we all know how to visualize the negative, the key
lies in using your talent to manifest your dharma, your
destiny, your dreams. Want to look further? Shakti
Gawain's book entitled *Creative Visualization* is well
worth you attention.

The Inspiration or breathing exercises alleviate stress
and tension so as to allow the mind to function without
hindrance or tether. The most powerful breathing drill-
and there are a few-is the simplest. (See Appendix)
    As you breathe in, draw your breath through your
nose, deep down into your lungs. It may feel like you are
drawing the air in to your stomach, that's good. Continue
to inhale until you feel all of your lung capacity, all the
way up to your collar bones, filled with air. Hold it for a

silent count of three, and then just relax.

Notice how the air rushes out and your lungs deflate of their own volition. This is the natural breath. Now it might, at first, not feel normal. You're right. It might be contrary to the way you have grown accustomed to breathing. Even so, stick with it. This breathing pattern might not-at first-seem normal, though it is most certainly natural. The way nature intended for you to breathe. Remember, the diaphragm is like any other muscle in the body. If it has not been used in a while, initially it will be stiff, weak and unresponsive. Stick with it. Progressively adapt the muscles of the respiratory system and your effort will be graciously rewarded.

This time, as you repeat the above, listen to the sound of your own inhale and exhale. Allow your mind to pay attention to the sound of your own breath. If your mind wanders off this natural mantra, simple and gently bring its attention back to the sound of your own inhale and exhale. Why not use your own breath as a mantra?

As for the nourishment aspect, page and time constraints prohibit a detailed discussion here. Should you choose to learn more about the optimal nourishment plan for the whole body including the mind, I strongly suggest both of the following books. *Brain Longevity* by Dharma Singh Khalsa, MD. and *8 Weeks to Optimal Health* by Andrew Weil. MD. Dr. Khalsa's book addresses many avenues for those interested in regaining their optimal mental function and health. Any time spent reading theses two talented physician/authors will serve you well. Their knowledge is a gracious gift.

Now the Deed or action portion of the Mind-Ups^{SM} are equally as simple. Movement of the body works wonders for the Mind. Walk outside in nature, breath in all the lessons she has to offer, move about as if you have already achieved your goal. As is the physical body, so is the mind. Remember Mr. Duffy, the bank cashier in James Joyce's *Dubliners*? He too "lived at a little distance form his body." Actively embrace all of who you are. Jump rope. Kick a stick. Fluidity and flexibility benefit one and all. Actions speak louder than words.

There is another mental fluidity which needs to be addressed. Forgive those with whom you hold a grudge, yourself included. Accept what happens to you, and with you, realizing that you are not the target of some cruel fate. Why not abandon the attempt to manipulate the outside world? Life is a challenge, welcome it as such. The flexibility to forgive is the greatest gift you can give yourself. Personally, my greatest lessons began the day I came to peace with my father. I forgave him and I forgave myself. Then-and only then-my Life began. Forgiveness, it's well worth the effort.

The Utilities portion of the Mind-Ups^{SM} address the "use or lose it" aspect of mental atrophy. Think of a unique way-right now-in which you may use your mind to "pump" mental iron. Think of a way to challenge yourself and progressively adapt your brain. Crossword puzzles, solitaire, drawing or maybe even working on a creative solution to a pressing problem, all of these are like push-ups for the brain.

From time to time, forget the calculator, do the math in your head. If you have the energy to hail a cab, you have the energy to walk. Plant a tree, walk the dog, dance a jig. Be creative. As in the mind, atrophy occurs in the body when you avoid actively living. When you shy away from life, you anesthetize mind and body alike. Why surrender your capacity to feel? Utilize your natural resources.. Drive your life, don't go along for the ride.

The Phase out category of the Mind-Ups^{SM} routine is one that needs no detailed explanation. When you actively employ the above steps and study the above mentioned books, you will soon begin to "phase out" the negative aspects of fear, loneliness, boredom, depression and stress. Live, celebrate, dance, sing and breath. We have these ailments in our life because we have chosen not to remove them. You will begin to phase these "habits" out of your life when you decide to follow your heart. Breathe, think and merry.

I challenge you to add Mind-Ups^{SM} to your list of push ups, sit ups and pull ups. Just as in the body, these exercises build strength, flexibility and endurance in the mind. In addition, they help to burn any "psychological fat" and reducing the plaque and build up of mental apathy, stress and fear.

Remember, stress, apathy and fear are not only destroyers of the body, they are killers of our dreams as well. Your brain/mind is your ultimate resource, your supreme present. Train it well and you will be rewarded.

In the end our search for *Something to Believe In* might have been called the Quest for Something to Know. For it is only when you directly experience yourself do you begin to learn about your overwhelming potential. To uncover your *dharma* and continually apply your natural resources, this is to be alive.

To surrender the formulated masks of laziness and conformity, to ignore the voices of *Chatterdom,* this is to be *in-lightened* as to your true potential. It's in there and you know it!

As George Bernard Shaw sees it: "This is the true joy in life, the being used for a purpose re-cognized by yourself as a mighty one; the being thoroughly worn out before you are thrown on the scrap heap..." and not a caretaker of the perpetual facade.

The only true joy in life will be felt when you employ your own natural resources in the *re-fulfillment* of your heart's desire. Should you seek an ordained value, let it come from there. Celebrate what you have always possessed. It is with this thought in mind that I leave you with the challenge of Guilliame Apolinarre:

"Come to the edge" he said.
They said, "NO, we are afraid."
"Come to the edge" he said.
They came. He pushed them
and they flew.

Ignore the conjectures and theories of the "experts." As

seductive as the Megaphone is-with its pageantry, pomp and circumstance-it is the magnifying glass that yields the only honest clues.

The models espoused by the telescope are impotent, the truths exposed by the microscope, robust and potent. The stethoscopic ear rings clear.

Educate yourself; and in doing so, you will soon begin to hear the faint, though *in-lightened* voice of the fundamental soul that lies within you. It is this whisper that will summon you to the edge of your own emptiness. Courageously push yourself and fly directly to the star that marks your heart. The Phoenix will rise from the ashes of your former facade.

"Close your eyes. Attend to the silence. Treasure the present. Embrace that which is offered here."

-THE WHISPER

APPENDIX

Inlightenment

•

There is a force within
Which gives you life—
seek that.
In your body
Lies a priceless gem—
Seek that.
O wandering Soul,
if you want to find the
Greatest Treasure
do not look outside,
Look inside, and seek that.

—RUMI

困

For centuries, the poets and philosophers of our world have written about the "dark night of the soul." When it was time to experience my own darkest night, its power surprised me. It was not a power that demanded my supplication. It did not attempt to strong arm or muscle me. Quite the contrary. Its potency and mastery were its simplicity.

The evening in the cemetery taught me many things. Most of the lessons communicated to by the whisper I have recanted for you. Even so, I have saved the greatest lesson for last. This lesson, oddly enough, was not taught to me by the voice. If there was a "teacher" at all it was nature herself. This is what I learned from her.

As I sat, propped against the tree, I watched as the clouds above me traveled across the moonlit sky. How effortlessly they floated on a current of wind. It did not matter to me that I could not see this wind. Its invisibility did not diminish its impact on either the clouds or me. In a whisp, the in-sight was clear. The same wind that fueled the clouds, powered my lungs. That wind and my breath had a common origin. I began to feel as if I could blow the clouds across the sky. I wondered if when I slept, did the sky return the favor. Was I breathing the wind or was the rushing breeze sustaining my life?

In Genesis, the original Hebrew uses the word "ruah" to describe the "rushing spirit of God." Now I am also told by a friend of mine who is a Rabbi that the word "ruah" has three distinctive translations; wind, spirit and breath. Upon re-cognizing this, it seems to imply that the Holy Spirit and the holy breath, are one and the same. You can be the judge. (In my upcoming book entitled The Theism of Breath, we discuss the comparative values of the worlds most prominent religions and how breath plays the same major role in each of them.) For now, I will focus on the Judeo-Christian religion if for no other reason other than the fact that it is the faith that I was born into and subsequently raised.

So far, at least according to Genesis, god is a breather. As he creates, he breathes. He calms chaos with his "rushing wind" just before creating the heavens and the earth. In a little while—less than a quarter of the chapter of Genesis—God creates humankind. First he created Adam by breathing "into his nostrils the breath of life." Then, when it was known that Adam could not survive without a female, what did God do? He caused Adam to fall into a deep sleep. (God told Adam that he (God) would take over Adam's breathing responsibilities for a the time.) While he slept, God removed a certain body part from Adam so to create Eve. Remember what it was?

Why would it be of any significance here? Good. God removed one of Adam's ribs, one of the bones that protects your lungs, right? Apparently, the lungs were an important enough organ for God to focus on when he created Eve. Should you decide to take a more evolutionary, scientific approach that's cool too. We never could have left the primordial swamps if we did not develop lungs.

Back to God. So for all the good parts in Genesis, God is a breather. He creates with his breath. He uses his diaphragm to get what he wants. So, if you were created in the image of your God, would you not also be a

Breather and Creator? As an aside, do you ever wonder why God created the Heaven(s) and not just a Heaven? Is it at all possible that your Heaven is within? There is only one earth in Genesis, yet there are multiple heavens. Did God breath life into multiple heavens and then create humankind to fill them? You decide.

Now, let's jump ahead. When Mosses is told by God to go forth to Egypt, Mosses asks the Lord, "Who shall I say sent me and God replies, "I am that I am" or I am what I do. God is saying to Mosses I am what I do. I am a breather. Do you find it at all interesting that God speaks to Mosses from a burning bush. In order for there to be a fire, there had to be oxygen. God's breath sustained the fire just as God's breath sustained Adam.

You and God speak the same language and that language is the breath. Ever wonder why the angels sing and blast their trumpets when they praise God. He understands the language of breath. Regardless of the dialect, the Almighty or the Supreme listens when you pray, that is to say God listens when you breathe. You want to talk to God? Breath!

Again we can address the difference between the normal breath—or the shallow chest breath that we are accustomed to—and the natural breath—that breath we used as infants. Ever watch an infant breath? Diaphragmatic breathing all the way, right? Ever wonder why the highest level of angels, the ones closest to God, are cherubim? Why do you suppose that when asked about gaining entrance to Heaven Jesus responded by saying that we must be like "children" to enter his father's house? Coincidence? You decide.

If you would like more information on the Mind-Ups[SM] Breathing techniques, e-mail me at mindwise 1@aol.com. Dr. Khalsa's book Brain Longevity and Dr. Weil's book 8 Weeks to Optimal Health are great resources also.

Until you have the opportunity to research any of the above resources, close your eyes, draw a breathe deep into your lungs, pay attention to your heart beat and just exhale. It saved my life and it will save yours.